PEBBLES,

MONOCHROMES,

and other

MODERN POEMS,

1891–1916

W. D. HOWELLS

PEBBLES,

MONOCHROMES,

and other

MODERN POEMS,

1891–1916

edited by EDWIN H. CADY

OHIO UNIVERSITY PRESS *Athens*

Ohio University Press, Athens, Ohio 45701
© 2000 by Edwin H. Cady
Printed in the United States of America
All rights reserved

Ohio University Press books are printed on acid-free paper ∞ ™

09 08 07 06 05 04 03 02 01 00   5 4 3 2 1

Library of Congress Cataloging-in-Publication Data
Howells, William Dean, 1837–1920.
    Pebbles, monochromes, and other modern poems,
        1891–1916 / W.D. Howells ; edited by Edwin H. Cady.
        p.   cm.
    Includes bibliographical references and index.
    ISBN 0-8214-1318-X (acid-free paper) —
    ISBN 0-8214-1319-8 (pbk. : acid-free paper)
        I. Cady, Edwin Harrison.   II. Title.

PS2030 .C33 2000
811'.4 — dc21   99-089155

CONTENTS

PREFACE

THOMAS F. O'DONNELL WAS ONE OF THE BEST graduate students I ever knew. He became an authority on Harold Frederic, editing the delightful "Frederic Herald," and an authority on the poetry of Howells with a contract to edit all the verse (1852–1916) for *The Selected Edition of W. D. Howells*. Catastrophically, when the federal funds subsidizing the Center of Editions of American Authors were stopped, O'Donnell's volume was among those that did not "make the cut" in the ensuing retrenchment. And at O'Donnell's too early death his widow was left with many boxes of papers on her hands. Included among them were the folders containing the materials for his edition.

Eventually Mrs. Gertrude O'Donnell deposited her late husband's papers in the J. B. Hubbell Archives and generously permitted me to use what proved helpful for my less extensive project. I offered to acknowledge every borrowing from them and hope both the texts and the "Notes" bear witness that the promise has been kept.

Next comes the pleasure of thanking readers and consultants like Thomas Wortham and John Tebbel, Polly Howells and Dorothy Oberhaus, Elizabeth Prioleau, Julia Lewis, Dorothy Bone, Louis Budd, David Nordloh, and Carol Lumia. My daughter Elizabeth Saler read and typed and encouraged. And, first and last, two from the dedicatory page cannot be "thanked" but still gratefully acknowledged. They all helped, but only I may take blame for the remaining errors and solecisms whatever they may be.

Finally there is the pleasant duty to acknowledge permissions to publish poems not previously printed. Professor William White Howells has granted me, for one use, author's copyrights to poems never before printed. Second, institutions have granted me permission to publish documents they own. Leslie A. Morris, Curator of Manuscripts, Houghton Library, Harvard University, on behalf of the Houghton Library gave one-time permission to use two unprinted poems by W. D. Howells with the shelf marks bMS Am 1784.2 (21) for the untitled poem "[Thomas Bailey Aldrich]" (see "Notes to the Poems" no. 66) and MS AM 1212.1 for "Aldrich, 1866–1907." Permission for "[To John Burroughs]" (see "Notes to the Poems" no. 62) comes from the William Dean Howells collection (#5651), Clifton Barrett Library, Special Collections Department, University of Virginia Library.

INTRODUCTION

W. D. HOWELLS CAPTURED NATIONAL ATTENTION as a professional author in 1860. To Boston and New York an Ohio poet was then "Western." He died in New York in 1920 internationally famous and a modernist.[1] For most of the first thirty years he wrote mainly as a Victorian American; but by 1890 he had grown into the modern tradition. Nothing better marks his modernity than the poems he began to write in 1889 or 1890 and published between 1891 and 1916. He announced the development in a letter to his father on November 3, 1890.[2] Not like his earlier verse, the new poetry showed the hand of an urban and modern poet. One of the most perceptive of Howells's contemporaneous appreciators called them "gravely beautiful and finely epigrammatic things," both "searching" and "modern."[3] Intrinsically, this edition of Howells's poetry, 1891–1916, collects, for the first time and in its best texts, a body of poetically significant work: poetry *qua* poetry, as used to be said. Extrinsically, the volume contributes both to general literary history and to the history of the modern tradition. It changes American literary history. It clarifies the biography of the poet and corrects the perspective in which the grounds for his reputation must be seen.

I

The first serious Howells scholar, who read all the work then between book covers, was Oscar W. Firkins. A

Harvard professor with a "Western" background himself, Firkins operated as a critic of the sort called "judicial" in his day. Condemning Howells's early poetry, Firkins found the work collected in *Stops of Various Quills* (1895) a "strange and wonderful thing, a revelation of the admirable potencies in Mr. Howells . . . to find originality, passion, power, genuineness, asserting themselves on the further side of middle life." This departure Firkins thought not matched by anything in American poetry. He said, "In poems like these we face the authentic power, depth, and weight of emotion converting itself into depth and weight of utterance by the rapid act of an aroused and potent imagination." The particular emotions, however, Firkins felt to be inexplicably sad, "almost without a counterpart in literature. . . . These poems . . . Come out of depths which American poetry has rarely plumbed." That mood, he said, distinguished Howells from Shelley, Keats, or Thomson, from Hardy and Maeterlinck.[4] Against that mood Howells had forewarned his father in 1890. Not everybody, however, responded to the dark tone of *Stops* so positively. Even Firkins concluded in doubt whether the "later poems will ever be justly rated: their bulk is small and their gloom does not prepossess." In a contemporaneous review, Harry Thurston Peck found that for him it certainly did not prepossess. He spoke of "intense" and "pervasive sadness." "It describes," he said, the "disillusion" of "one whose nerves are overstrained, whose spirit is sickened, and whose very soul is sorrowful and despairing."[5] That was, in the 1890s, the sort of language hostile critics employed to discipline "decadents."

Howells's "pessimism" nevertheless rooted itself in common earth. He became intimate with the mystery of its pain, and, though other events and experiences broadened his knowledge, the deep thrust came from the tragic death of his daughter Winifred in 1889. That set off his explosion into a new poetry. Poems published between 1891 and 1904 answer to that stroke of fate. None is franker than "Change" (1894):

> Sometimes, when after spirited debate
>> Of letters or affairs, in thought I go
>> Smiling unto myself, and all aglow
> With some immediate purpose, and elate
> As if my little trivial scheme were great,
>> And what I would so were already so:
>> Suddenly I think of her who died, and know,
> Whatever friendly or unfriendly fate
>> Befall me in my hope or in my pride,
> It is all nothing but a mockery,
> And nothing can be what it used to be,
>> When I could bid my happy life abide,
> And build on earth for perpetuity,
>> Then, in the deathless days before she died.

The worst of having to endure Winifred's death was not the stark fact alone. It would have been bad enough for her parents to lose their eldest, the baby of their Venetian honeymoon, their gifted and charming child: as Henry James wrote, "to be young and gentle and do no harm, and only to pay for it as if it were a crime."[6] A long background of suffering, invalidism, and decline, a path of doom nine years long tortured Winifred and of course her parents. Even worse, they were persuaded to become complicit in multiplying her pain. The relatively primitive medicine of the 1880s, unequipped to diagnose aright, thought her disease must be psychic, even "moral." Physicians thought it must be something like neurasthenia or hypochondria or hysteria, a disease of the will to be cured by discipline to override her "stubborn" insistence that her pain was real. After more than eight years of agony and failing "treatment," in a last effort Howells sent Winifred to his friend the most famous of American alienists, Dr. S. Weir Mitchell. At Mitchell's sanitarium she "improved" until suddenly on March 2, 1889, she died.

Still worse, worst, upon autopsy Mitchell apparently discovered a real and organic disease that had caused her pain and at last her death.[7] On being told that fact, Howells answered Mitchell's report: "The torment that remains is that perhaps the poor child's pain was all along as great as she fancied, if she was so diseased, as apparently she was." The effect on the Howellses, as he wrote his father, was "anguish, anguish that rends the heart and brain."[8] Though the parents could not have avoided Winifred's death, they had been duped into a long collaboration in her isolation and suffering. Small wonder that Howells admired Charlotte Perkins Gilman's "The Yellow Wallpaper," persuaded his friend Edwin D. Mead to print it, and included it in his anthology of *Great Modern American Short Stories* (1920). No such mystery as Firkins supposed informed the dark woe of Howells's later poems.

How did he find time to write poems? To survive, he had to ride out the storm of creativity that possessed him. When did he write them? Perhaps in bursts in 1889–90, in 1891, and again in 1894–95. There is no way to be sure; but as he told St. Loe Strachey later, the poems of 1890–95 expressed "all that was most serious in my life at one time."[9] As William Blake proposed, Howells did "not cease from Mental Fight" but only increased his warfare for justice and for esthetic sanity. He plunged into metaphysical and religious reflection, though it always concluded in mystery. And he developed an ethics of self-abnegation which owed as much to his father's Swedenborgianism as to Tolstoy. In these directions the new poetry became metaphysical. It studied guilt and dread and tragic irony. For instance, the concluding poem of the magazine gathering "Stops of Various Quills" (1894):

CONSCIENCE

Judge me not as I judge myself, O Lord!
  Show me some mercy, or I may not live:
Let the good in me go without reward;
  Forgive the evil I must not forgive!

II

The titles Howells gave to gatherings of poems published in *Harper's Monthly* before the collection called *Stops of Various Quills* (1895) catch at one's attention. Those titles— "Moods," "Monochromes," "Pebbles," and the set implied by subtitles, "Impressions"—were modernist. *Stops of Various Quills* as a title looked back to Victorian elegance. To quote

"Lycidas" was to regress. Instinctively one blames the Harpers: surely *they* had not imagined modernist titles. Perhaps Howells thought of "Lycidas" himself, though not improbably Henry Mills Alden, for the Harpers, suggested that he consider propriety. Perhaps there was a sort of deal, letting Howells say "Pebbles" in the magazine if the volume title quoted Milton. As Thomas F. O'Donnell pointed out, the "Lycidas" contexts nevertheless imply a richness. The context from the last paragraph of "Lycidas" reads:

Thus sang the uncouth swain to the th'oaks and rills,
While the still morn went out with sandals gray;
He touched the tender stops of various quills,
With eager thought warbling his Doric lay;
And now the sun had stretched out all the hills,
And now was dropped into the western bay;
At last he rose, and twitched his mantle blue:
Tomorrow to fresh woods and pastures new.

"Doric" suggests rustic and direct—Spartan music. Howells too had made it fresh and new and made it courageous, and rough-textured. As a good Miltonist, O'Donnell knew enough to look further into Milton and find the full effect. "Dorian" appears again in Book I of *Paradise Lost*. By line 549 Satan has roused his crushed host of fallen angels from their stupor on the floor of hell. Reformed as troops,

Anon they move
In perfect phalanx to the Dorian mood

Of flutes and soft recorders; such as raised
To height of noblest temper heroes old
Arming to battle, and instead of rage
Deliberate valor breathed. . .

There was, if one knew Milton, not a genteel but a militant subtext to the title *Stops of Various Quills*. Howells proposed to fight, mainly to use irony as his weapon, and so Milton's "Doric" fitted his mood. For practical use, however, the modernist "Pebbles," more radical, more immediate in impact, would have been better. The poet's feel for his work was more modern than Miltonic.

All during the decade around *Stops of Various Quills* Howells engaged strenuously in his version of Blake's "Mental Fight." To read the poetry requires understanding of its place in a large warfare the poet simultaneously waged on other fronts. He battled for democracy: literary, economic, caste, class, political, and personal. A torrent of creativity flowed into Howells's fight. It seems warrantable to suppose that he began writing the poetry published in and around "Moods" and "Monochromes" in 1889 while *A Hazard of New Fortunes* was appearing in *Harper's Weekly*. In March 1890 *The Shadow of a Dream* began in *Harper's Young People;* every month through March 1892, "The Editor's Study" column came out. In 1891 appeared *Criticism and Fiction*, with serialization of *An Imperative Duty* starting in July and in October *The Quality of Mercy* as syndicated by S. S. McClure. March 1892 saw the end of "The Editor's Study" but in November came the first of the

Altrurian sketches, which would not cease until October 1893, with *A Traveller from Altruria* published as a book in May 1894. All this amid a shower of autobiography, farces, short stories, important radical essays, lasting through 1895.

Surprisingly in view of traditions about the gentle and "genteel" Howells, much of this torrent of production sprang from veins of anger. Howells himself stands witness and in 1890 he confessed repeatedly. Of George William Curtis he said: "There is a man of a wholly different make from me: he does good because he loves; I because I hate"; and he confided to Edward Everett Hale that "I am all the time stumbling to my feet from the dirt of such falls through vanity and evil will, and hate, that I can hardly believe in that self that seems to write books which help people." These things were said in thanks for praise of *A Hazard of New Fortunes,* and by then Howells must have composed the poems of "Moods" and "Monochromes." To the Boston sculptress Anne Whitney he wrote, "I am afraid that I hate the wrong more than I love the right."[10]

What he hated was the infliction of human pain: the ironist in him, long practiced, ached to scarify it. When did he first cite Tennyson's line from "The Princess" about "the riddle of the painful earth," the mystery of evil as pain? He believed, as a key scene in *The Rise of Silas Lapham* had put it, in a principle of "the economy of pain." Be parsimonious with pain. Cause and let cause in the world as little pain as you can. A bedrock moral principle, that idea informed much of the poetry after 1890. Within him creative impulses arose from preconscious depths of pain and hate (and therefore alienation), but also from guilt and penitence for the hatred, and from bewilderment (and displacement of sensibility) in face of the mystery. Here lie evidences not of evil intent but of an exceedingly tender conscience. As one result, a tone of woe darkled through the new poetry. "Solitude" provides an apparently simple but finally quite complex example:

> Ah, you cannot befriend me with all your love's tender
> persistence:
> In your arms' pitying clasp sole and remote I remain,
> Rapt as far from help as the last star's measureless distance,
> Under the spell of our life's innermost mystery, Pain!

III

Living in Cambridge, Massachusetts, where he had gone to work as assistant editor of the *Atlantic Monthly*, Howells found a constellation of fine minds of his own generation. Social life was as intense in that group as the intellectual life, and he made friends of John Fiske, Henry Adams, T. S. Perry, and, above all, William and Henry James. These all helped lead American thought into the modern in their generation. Their ideas were pluralistic, antiromantic, agnostic, pragmatic, realistic. Nevertheless they stayed humane. Their followers would be figures like Stephen Crane, Frank Norris, E. A. Robinson, Robert Frost. It was typical of William James, psychologist and philosopher, friend of thirty years' standing, that at New Year's 1895 he should write about the gathering "Stops of Various Quills":

Dear Old Howells:

I have just been reading your verses in the December Harper, and don't know when I have had a greater pleasure —if pleasure is the word for so solid a sense of gratitude. They are well forged—no fumbling and no spatter, and I do hope that with others of their predecessors they shall be "collected" soon.

You're a weighty phenomenon, taking length, breadth, depth, and superficial area all into account. I can't well expatiate to a man about himself, but I do feel solemn and affectionate towards you; and the New Year's tide allows of such messages as this. So here's a God bless you, you and yours.[11]

Prepared by experience as much as affection, James registered Howells's anguish and struggle and responded perfectly. James already held citizenship in Altruria, the ideal commonwealth of which Howells had just been writing. There women and men lived for one another, not on one another. James was modern but compassionate. So was Howells.

To be, then, humane was one of the ways to be modern. Ellmann and Feidelson found that the perplexities in defining modernism drove them to paradox and pluralism. Looking back from the postmodern we speak in the plural of modernisms. So Howells's modernism was of the humane sort, and the younger generation he cultivated were of the same sort. Both in Boston and the pulsating New York to which he moved late in 1891, the young and radical flocked about Howells: for instance, Cahan, Crane, Dunbar, Garland, Herne, and Norris. But the most exotic bird to fly to Howells, perch, and fly away was the bilingual poet Stuart Merrill. Howells's relationship with him illustrates a great deal about his nexus to modernism. Merrill would have fascinated Henry James. He extraordinarily represented the rich American poised between two cultures. The extraordinary qualities in him were powers of intellect and sensibility. Horrified by the human condition under modern industrial and urban circumstances, Merrill was too humane to distance himself in cynicism or despair. He became what we now call an activist.

Hardly more than a year after Winifred's death, Howells dated his introduction to a new book "April 1890." The book was entitled *Pastels in Prose* and was an anthology, edited and translated by Stuart Merrill, of French prose sketches by figures like Baudelaire, Huÿsmans, Mallarmé, and Villiers de L'Isle-Adam. Merrill had obviously become at an early age an accepted member of the *Symbolistes*. He persuaded three authors to write expressly for his volume of prose poems, talked a widow into selecting examples from her deceased husband's unpublished manuscripts for him, and got two men to let him pick from the proof-sheets of volumes yet in press. Born on Long Island in 1863 the child of wealth, Merrill was reared and educated in France. Precocious to the point of brilliance, he joined the esthetic revolt led by William Morris and the *Symbolistes,* entering the movement on both its decorative and its humanitarian sides. He began to publish poetry in French and to associate with *Symboliste* friends before completing his degree of *bachelier ès lettres* in 1884. If Merrill's father thought he would put a stop to all that by returning to New York and putting Merrill in Columbia Law School, father guessed wrong. Merrill went on writing good *Symboliste* poetry. He published in Paris a first volume in 1887 and a second volume, *Les fastes* (1893), which was dedicated to W. D. Howells.

In America Stuart Merrill plunged into the campaign of social protest. He worked so hard for Henry George that his father disowned him. When Howells stood in effect alone to plead the cause of the Chicago Anarchists, Merrill stepped to his side. Howells found Merrill's "Pastels" to be "peculiarly modern" and demonstrative of "the most courageous faith in art, the finest respect for others, the wisest self-denial. . . ." Merrill bespoke the best of the modern and humane. And he helped W. D. Howells, at the beginning of the 1890s when he was composing a new poetry, to espouse the "peculiarly modern." One wonders whether Merrill's "Pastels" suggested "Monochromes" to Howells.

If Howells espoused the symbolist "Pastels" not just out of gratitude and sympathy but also with the hope of keeping Merrill in his native country, however, he failed. In 1892, on Merrill's way back to France, a note reached his ocean liner just before sailing. It came from W. D. Howells: "B. tells me you are going abroad for a year. I want you to be an American poet and to write in English. A man is not born in his country for nothing. I wish I might persuade you." But Merrill sailed away to become a humane *Symboliste,* a permanent fixture in the literature of France.[12] That was a part of Howells's bad luck with a generation of lost followers: Merrill went home to France; Frederic, Crane, and Frank Norris died young.

IV

Howells spent most of the summer of 1890 in the Adirondacks, and was probably at Lake Placid in July when Mabel Loomis Todd came to show him poems by Emily Dickinson and tell him about that strange life. If Todd came to persuade him to review the first volume of *Poems* scheduled for publication in November, she succeeded. His review from advance proofs was ready by October for publication in the January 1891 "Editor's Study" column of *Harper's Monthly*. In short, he read Emily Dickinson before he showed his father the lines of "Moods" if not "Monochromes."

In maturity he tended to respond to "influences" much in the way to which he pointed when he remarked to Arthur Hobson Quinn that he had felt not inspired but authorized by the French novel. But it was not surprising that he called Dickinson's *Poems* "a distinctive addition to the literature of the world." He did not fail to mark in Dickinson that, "Occasionally, the outside of the poem, so to speak, is left so rough, so rude, that the art seems to have faltered. But there is apparent to reflection the fact that the artist meant just this hard exterior to remain. . . ." Here stood authorization for prosodic practice like that evident in "Moods" and "Monochromes" and "Pebbles," for a modernist poetics. Some of the best poems Howells had written or was gestating when he came to read Emily Dickinson concerned death. Of course in 1890 he could not keep the subject away. Such "Moods" as

"Life" and "Living" and such "Monochromes" as "Question," "The Bewildered Guest," and "If" stand among the best he wrote. Certainly they were authorized by the Dickinson he reviewed. His review quoted in full ten things from her *Poems;* and five of these were, as he said, "mortuary."[13] From neither poet's sensibility could the other's poems have risen. Yet Dickinson might well have felt authorized by Howells had she read "Monochromes"; and he did read her.

There is also evidence to suggest that a line of authorization ran from Dickinson through Howells to Stephen Crane, who spoke of his own poems as "pills." Under the ministrations of Hamlin Garland, Crane had undergone a sort of conversion experience beginning in 1891. The inscription in Howells's copy of *The Red Badge of Courage* read: "To W. D. Howells this small and belated book as a token of the veneration and gratitude of Stephen Crane for many things he has learned of the common man and, above all, for a certain re-adjustment of his point of view victoriously concluded some time in 1892. Stephen Crane." It could hardly be questioned whether Crane followed intently whatever Howells published. He could not have omitted the new poetry appearing in *Harper's.* When Howells, who liked *Maggie, A Girl of the Streets,* invited Crane to tea, Crane responded some time close to the first of April 1893. "Monochromes" had just been published in the March *Harper's.* Naturally they must have appealed to Crane and afforded him a topic of conversation. John D. Barry, who edited the magazine *Forum,* was a friend of both Howells and

Crane; and he testified (though ten years later) that at that tea Howells read to Crane poems by Emily Dickinson and that Crane almost immediately began to produce his own first poetry. That is to suggest that Crane read "Monochromes" and discussed them with Howells, who thereupon read Emily Dickinson to him. Crane's authority for beginning what would become *The Black Riders* was, then, double: Howells and Dickinson.[14] It costs little effort to group poems by the three to illustrate how they speak to one another, for instance Dickinson's "I shall know why, when time is over" and Howells's "If" and Crane's "A youth in apparel that glittered." Though the voices and legends differ radically, the ironies of death and dreaming work out in parallel. Each might be used to authorize the others.

It was with the contents of *Stops of Various Quills,* Howells told his old friend E. C. Stedman, that "I came fullest to my poetic consciousness."[15] Of what, then, was he newly conscious? Most of the answer may be inferred from the verse; and the character of his poetics consists a great deal in what they were not. His new idea stood in opposition to the notions with which he and poet friends like Aldrich and Stedman had begun (and they continued). The poetics of Howells's youth had looked mainly to Tennyson and Longfellow, but his new prosody left Aldrich and Stedman in the past. Howells set the point firmly in praise he wrote for Langdon E. Mitchell's *Poems* in 1894. He applauded in Mitchell "what I should call honesty; the things seem really to have been felt and thought too." And,

he added, "there is a manly tone, with that occasional rough-
ness of voice which you intended, in every poem, that make me
glad of your company."[16]

It must not, however, be imagined that the poet of "Pebbles"
and "Monochromes" liked "rough" poetic voice because he
could not write musically. To say nothing about the poetry of
his youth, the musicality of some of his twentieth-century
writing proves otherwise. In "The City and the Country . . ."
the "country mouse" urges the charms of a New England
Indian Summer:

> I tell you, it is gay
> Down here. You ought to see the Hunter's Moon,
> These silver nights, prinking in our lagoon.
> You ought to see our sunsets, glassy red,
> Shading to pink and violet overhead.
> You ought to see our mornings, still and clear,
> White silence, far as you can look and hear.
> You ought to see the leaves—our oaks and ashes
> Crimson and yellow, with those gorgeous splashes,
> Purple and orange, against the bluish green
> Of the pine woods; and scattered in between,
> The scarlet of the maples; and the blaze
> Of blackberry-vines, along the dusty ways
> And on the old stone walls; the air just balm,
> And the crows cawing through the perfect calm
> Of afternoons all gold and turquoise.

And in "The Mother" the title character thinks of common solace for the baby she has been imagining as trailing clouds of glory from a lost home in heaven. In this world too there are consolations, and the musicality of "The Mother" moderates into a different palette of tone colors:

> The life of earth, it seems so beautiful,
> Far more than anything imaginable
> Of any life elsewhere. They cannot hear
> Anything like the crowing of the cocks
> In heaven—so drowsy and so drowsing! Hark,
> How thin and low and faint it is! Oh, sweet,
> They keep on calling in their dim, warm barns,
> With the kind cattle underneath their roosts,
> Munching the hay, and sighing rich and soft.
> I used to hear it when I was a child,
> And now those things they seem to call me back,
> And claim my life a part of theirs again.
> I hope that she will live to love such things,
> Dear simple things of our dear simple earth.

Howells's voicing admits of modern dissonances. But there is nothing rough about this music.

His aim in poetry as in fiction was now to avoid what he called the "literose" (the making of literature out of previous literature rather than felt life). He joined poetry now to his realistic positions. He had explained things to a young stranger who wrote in appreciation of "Monochromes" in 1893: *"The*

Monochromes [*sic*] came from a mood of mine that was very genuine, and I am glad that they appealed to you as good pieces of realism; it is hard for people to understand that realism excludes nothing that is true."[17] As in fiction Howells thought romantic styles should be toned down, he had come to like poetry, including his poetry, roughened in texture: "the meal in the firkin, the milk in the pan," Emerson had said in his essay "The Poet." But Emerson also held that "it is not metres, but a metre-making argument that makes a poem—a thought so passionate and alive that . . . it has an architecture of its own." Much like Emerson, but precisely without platonism, Howells proposed to answer organically to the passion of his thought and in verse be free with everything but rhyme. *Vers libre* offended Howells who rejected it, even in his much-admired Stephen Crane, as "too orphic for me." Nevertheless, the prosodies of his own verse were mightily liberated. The result appears as favorably in the three "Impressions" of 1891–94 as anywhere.

The later Howells's prosodic practice has become liberated and thus experimental. Meters scan, or they scan loosely, or they do not scan. Regularities come and go. Much the same holds true for patterns of rhyme: he rhymed exactly or roughly or sometimes distantly. His ear favored triplets. He fancied heroic couplets but experimented with them in ways that Alexander Pope would have thought "Gothick." He sometimes mixed iambic pentameters with trimeter, even dimeter, lines. His verse could not be called "free," but it was sometimes freer than Emerson's. Much the same holds true for the fourteen sonnets he wrote in those latter years. They range from lawful to outlaw in form but include some of his best poems, for instance "The Bewildered Guest" as against "Twelve P.M."

By 1916, however, the paeans that resounded in the press for *The Daughter of the Storage* must have rather surprised Howells. The book intercalated sketches and tales with the five major narrative poems gathered under "Scene and Story" in this volume. Admiring the deliberate roughening of verses in Dickinson and Langdon Mitchell, Howells had refused to admire *vers libre*. But now he found the *New York Times* (2 April 1916) lost in admiration for what it insisted on calling Howells's *vers libre*, "for lack of a better term." And, it added, "There is surely an effect produced by these rhymed and unrhymed forms of verse . . . a sort of glamour difficult to define, but at which the author must have aimed, and which might not be evoked by any other form of expression." That was, in essence, what Howells had said about Dickinson.

V

Having produced the contents of *Stops* by 1894 or early 1895, Howells's poetic muse shut down for something like three years. When she opened shop again she returned in another mood. Now she gazed outward, a more public muse. The writer she controlled was already well practiced in narrative and playwrighting. He excelled in farce and other modes of public irony. "Scene and Story" as a title covers the most and best of his excellent and little-known verses written after 1897.

The first of this poetry emerged as "Breakfast Is My Best Meal." As the subtitle says, it was inspired by the experience of a "cure" at Carlsbad. Worn down especially by the rigors of a lecture tour, he caved in to his doctor's suggestion that he go "take" the tepid, smelly waters. That very European experience made him feel very American and Middle Western. He took his revenge in "Breakfast Is My Best Meal." It is not in dialect so much as Midwestern vernacular, and it scored a fine popular success.

Except that they are laid in a "village house," the three "Dramatic Passages" about a "Father" and a "Mother" represent something altogether different. Not consecutively, Howells wrote a triad of dialogues in sophisticated blank verse. The triad, to consider the poems together, might have been called "Marriage: Theme and Variations." But I think that until Howells reached the third poem, "After the Wedding," he gave no thought to combining the three, and the effort in 1909 to join them into the semblance of a drama failed.

The Mother and the Father somewhat resemble Basil and Isabel March, who recur through six of Howells's fictions, much more than they resemble Howells and his wife. The "Dialogues" are also fiction, not autobiography. For instance, Winifred was born in a Venetian palazzo, was not an only child and never married, and she died in a sanitorium as far from village conditions as the palazzo. But the daughter of these poems is born in a "village house," is married in it and buried from it. No such setting presented itself in Winifred's life. Nevertheless, of course, the death of Winifred haunted her father's imagination, as such poems as "Sorrow, my Sorrow" and "Experience" record.

"Mystery" belonged to the original title and can be dropped only at the peril of losing part of the poem's force. "Mystery" of course has multiple implications. Death is a mystery and life after death, a matter of faith, also. When the question of life after death extends itself to spiritualism, another mystery arises. Not a sacramental mystery as in the medieval mystery play, here is a still contemporary question: does a human spirit live after the death of the body and, if so, can that spirit by any means communicate to those still in the flesh? Howells knew people convinced of the truth of spiritualism and many others convinced of its falsity. He knew agnostics like William James who did not believe but insisted that spiritualist claims must be soberly, scientifically researched. Howells's novel *The Undiscovered Country* (1880) had rejected spiritualism as delusive and fraudulent. After Winifred's death he dabbled briefly in spiritualism but with disillusioning results. At last "The Father and the Mother: A Mystery" presents not a mystery play but, agnostically, a mystery dramatic passage that ends in an enigma of dubiety: but one cannot leave the mystery out.

The 1909 volume, however, started off with "The Mother" (of 1902) and got the baby born. Next came "After the Wedding" (of 1906); at last, with a show of balance, "The Father" (1900) (no "Mystery") concludes. *The Mother and the Father* is nicely bound, illustrated, and padded out with a wealth of white space to make a volume of fifty-five pages. Including the same 1909 text in his edition of *The Complete Plays of William Dean Howells* (1960), Walter Meserve compressed it all into eleven and a third pages. Meserve admits that what he calls the "trilogy" is not a play but wishes to claim it "because it reveals a depth and poetry of soul in Howells unparalleled in his other dramatic works" (561). It seems an oblique excuse for trying to preempt among "Plays" the best of Howells's blank verse poems. Precedents for "closet drama" written not to be played but read abounded in Victorian poetry, which is the reason why Howells thought of "Dramatic Passages." But each of these poems stands on its feet. Originally nothing suggested the dramatic unities of plot or development. To put them in the order of the 1909 book suggests something repellent to the thought of W. D. Howells: what is the history of woman? Born, married, dead. His art like his discursive ideas suggests everything else; and things the Mother says work out to a feminism condemnatory of every such littleism. That and not the other was Howells.

Almost everything applicable to "Father and Mother: A Mystery" applied to "The Mother." Its locus, "the upper chamber of a village house," not at all a Venetian palazzo, distances all notions of reference to the birth of Winifred Howells or to Howells's own fatherly experience. On the other hand, Howells had grown up in a philoprogenitive and baby-loving family and transferred the same fatherly warmth to his own children. The nervous, befuddled Father in "The Mother" was not at all Howells. But the prize portrait of the poem became that of the naturally ambivalent Mother, swinging with her feelings from transcendental speculations to the "Dear simple things of our dear simple earth." She perfectly represents what Howells had said of the Edwardian woman: not Chaucer's

"Patient Griselda," she had become an "Impatient Grizzle." "The Mother" deserves the praise of Mark Twain's cordial Christmas Eve, 1902, letter to Howells: "deeply moving."

"After the Wedding," last published of the triad, had to be placed second for the verisimilitude of the 1909 volume. That became the more awkward in that the Mother now wishes to defy the elements of transcendental idealism she had voiced in the earlier poem. For her the Father's agnosticism has translated itself into unbelief. As she says: "Women must have some faith or other / They cannot halt half-way in yes and no." And the Wordsworthian idea of the child has become a "shattered fantasy."

And she has some plain feminist things to say to her husband after he incautiously cites "nature":

> "Nature! How you men
> Are always talking about Nature! Little
> You understand her! Nature flatters men.
> She gives them mastery and health and life,
> And women subjection, weakness, pain and death.
> We know what Nature is, and you know nothing.
> She takes our youth and wastes it upon you,
> She steals our beauty for you, and she uses
> Our love itself to enslave us to you. Nature!"

In short, the "Dramatic Passages" really closed on a set of modernist chords.

Much the same is true of "City and Country: A Long-distance Eclogue." It emerges as a modern comic pastoral with a lineage. To Howells early in the twentieth century its mode returned from deep in his extraordinary self-education. In the winter of 1851–52 Howells's family sojourned in Columbus, Ohio. By day young Will, fourteen, worked as child labor at setting type; but he spent his evenings "producing and polishing" a pastoral poem after the manner of Alexander Pope: "a plaster-of-paris masterpiece," he said autobiographically. Apparently never finished, that enterprise instructed the boy in the tradition of the pastoral. With ancient beginnings in Theocritus and Virgil, the pastoral marched with an army of disciples down through Shelley and Matthew Arnold to Robert Frost and W. H. Auden. It is no doubt alive and well today.

Fifty years after his youthful experiment, Howells found that the humorous potentialities of the ancient mode stirred his creative juices. By 1902 he had often exploited associations accrued to the famous mode. It had shifted shapes many times, often into debates that grew traditions of their own. Which is better: the country or the city? the imperial court or the farm? the sophisticated East or the wholesome West? Europe or America? the Ancient or the Modern? the Machine or the Human? the mercantile or the agrarian? the Hamiltonian or the Jeffersonian?

Politically in a broad sense, Howells had generally come down on the Jeffersonian side. But now he was out for comedy. The swains of Columbus, "Clorinda" and "Daphnis," had aged into Morrison and Wetherbee, veteran New York clubmen. And the first part of the fun was to put Clorinda/Morrison and Daphnis/Wetherbee to shouting on the long-distance phone between Clamhurst Shortsands and Manhattan. As to the substance of the conversation, were it supposed that rough old Howells could not write lyric nature poetry, Morrison's celebration of the beauties of autumnal New England would lay the doubt to rest. Yet, with full allowance for the nuisances of urban life, Wetherbee wins the debate for Dr. Johnson. It's striking entertainment.

One of the best single touchstones for Howells's modernity is "Black Cross Farm," first published in England in 1904. It could be slipped into Robert Frost's *North of Boston* (1914) or *Mountain Interval* (1916) without occasioning alarm to a nonspecialist. Something of the same might be true for E. A. Robinson's *The Town Down the River* (1910). Like many a Robinson or Frost poem, "Black Cross Farm" deals in the riddle of the painful earth, in bewilderment at the loss of the New England past, in dissociation and alienation, in lostness. The metrics of the poem look simple—heroic couplets, but Howells complicated them in a direction Frost liked: toward the sound of speech. Howells is seldom given enough credit for the virtuosities of his command of style. Writing for money every day, year in and year out, decade after decade, he developed a Bach-like dexterity. It is hard to think of any way he could not write. When in 1915 Howells reviewed *A Boy's Will* and *North of Boston,* he pleased Frost by grasping the essence of what he called the "strong, sweet music . . . though it does not always keep step (wilfully breaks step at times, we should say), but always remains faithful to the lineage of poetry that danced before it walked."[18] Frost paid his debt in a posthumous tribute addressed to Hamlin Garland. Howells,

Frost said, "wrote beautiful blank verse." Yet, he continued, "My obligation to him is not for the particular things he did in verse form, but for the perennial poetry of all his writings in all forms. I learned from him a long time ago that the loveliest theme of poetry was the voices of people. No one ever had a more observing ear or clearer imagination for the tones of those voices. No one ever brought them more freshly to book."[19]

Observations like that point us past the metrics to the music and voicing of "Black Cross Farm." For the most part these belong to the narrator. And they speak a self-deprecating, self-mocking sound of sense. There is a playful, almost Chaucerian tonality:

> The right way was to happen, as they did,
> Upon it in the hills where it was hid;
> But chance could not always be trusted, quite,
> You might not happen on it, though you might. . . .
> The next best thing that we could do
> Was in his carry-all, to start together.
> And trust . . .

It's a lark, likely enough a wild goose chase. And yet it's a quest, too, for the mysterious: to seek "Black Cross Farm" becomes a pilgrimage—maybe blessed, maybe not.

Synecdoche takes a modernist hand in the indeterminacy here. We go a-questing—but maybe not to a Dark Tower, maybe down the famous country road that starts fair, becomes a wagon trace, then one path, then a blazed trail, and at last runs up a tree as a squirrel track. And need anybody care? asks the chuckle of the narrator. That bucolic mood runs clear through line 75 and the accidental finding of the gate. As synecdoche it speaks of alienation from the pastness of a bygone culture. Playful voicing quarrels ironically with the sense of lostness; and there is as yet no revelation promised even in the mock joy of the friend's ultimate cry, "Oh, here we are! At last! At last!" Where are we? Out in the woods and next to nowhere. With the images of deserted old houses, cemetery, orchards, a synecdoche familiar to Frost appears; and the voicing darkens. Here is the synecdoche of the deserted homestead proper to a culture mourner. Now the narrator is not far from Yeats or Hardy or Frost. He has filiations to early T. S. Eliot. The synecdochal connections of the deserted house doubtless reach back to the childhood of the human race.

But there is more about the deserted house to be discovered. It stands in ". . . a space / Shaped as by Nature for the dwelling-place / Of kindly human life: a small plateau / Open to the heaven that seemed bending low / In liking for it." Some sort of *genius loci,* some domestic natural teleology appears to cherish the site. Nature can be right for human life. And the house, worn by the generations, is still viable: "So clean and cold . . . / So lifelike and so deathlike, with the thrill / Of hours when life and death encountered still / Passionate in it." All but those in the graveyard have left, and no hint of explanation exists. Life has gone away in a mystery. Though there is scarcely time to register the fact until every other fact is overwhelmed by the greatest, both a mystery and either a synecdoche or the edge of one may be glimpsed as the narrator looks back from the graves. "The house was old . . . but the barn, gray and vast, / Stood new and straight and strong." Whoever deserted the place had prospered at farming and left anyhow. Nothing tells the tale, especially in dairy country, like a new barn.

But the dairy business vanishes at the impact of the second perception of the new barn standing by the fine old house on the site apparently designed for human life. I think it important to notice what the narrator registers as he sees it. "Turning, my heart was pierced with more intense / Suggestion of a mystical dismay." Though the narrator has just been playing with Gothic notions of ghosts in the old house and the melancholy of "the moss-grown names upon the tombs," all playfulness vanishes at his second glance, hence the force of "more intense." The language proceeds with care. Though emotion is strong—"my heart was pierced"—yet neither faith nor assenting religious experience follows; he is a modern man pierced with the "Suggestion of a mystical dismay." As "pierced" and "mystical" might speak from an Age of Faith, "suggestion" and "dismay" flat their tones for an Age of Unfaith. For on the sheathing of the hay-mow, sealing the opening, "A Cross was nailed, the bigness of a man, / Aslant from left to right . . . / And painted black as paint could make it."

Symbol or synecdoche, there stood a key to the question: why were home and farm deserted? There stood the key, but what lock did it open? The answer failed. A volley of questions to the guide elicits agnostic responses: nobody knows, there is no name; the folk tell no legend; no evidence appears. All enquiry has drawn a blank. The gravestones lead to nothing. Pressed, however, the friend confesses to a humanistic theory. In an Age of Unfaith, the symbols of bygone Faith still express conditions of the human heart. He says,

> "Suppose
> That some one that had known the average woes
> Of human nature, finding that the load
> Was overheavy for him on life's road,
> Had wished to leave some token in this Cross,
> Of what had been his gain and been his loss,
> Of what had been his suffering and of what
> Had also been the solace of his lot?
> Whoever that unknown brother-man might be,
> I think he must have been like you and me,
> Who bear our Cross, and when we fail at length,
> Bow down and pray to it for greater strength."

The narrator applauds indeterminacy as "better" than a known "tragedy . . . which were / In being the more definite the vulgarer." So they turn to leave "the mystery to the summer day" and, lost going as they were coming, grope their way back to the horse. The past can only tell them it too suffered the riddle of the painful earth. At last, diminuendo: "all the wayside scenes reversing, we / Dropped to the glimpses of the distant sea, / Content as if we brought, returning thus, / The secret of the Black Cross back with us." Needless to say, the ironic last line underscores the presumption that nobody ever will know the secret. It is rare enough, hard enough even to see

XXXIX

and contemplate its relics, more runic than Christian. Failing the secret, however, there can be no harm in reading it in the mirror of Howells's known ideas.

No philosopher, Howells the artist never analyzed or systematized ideas. Having felt their force, he dramatized them. To the principle of the economy of pain, he added the idea of complicity (everybody is somehow guilty of every wrong) first in *The Minister's Charge* (1882). Next came the idea of solidarity (in life and death every human being is bound to each and all others) in *Annie Kilburn* (1889) and *A Hazard of New Fortunes* (1890). Lastly, an idea of humanistic vicarious atonement (the suffering of the good may atone for the evil done by the wicked). Atonement appears as a closing idea in *A Hazard of New Fortunes* but it is more clearly stated at the end of *The Son of Royal Langbrith* (1905), which Howells probably had in work when he wrote "Black Cross Farm." In Langbrith, speaking of a cruel scoundrel, the Episcopalian Rev. Mr. Enderby asks:

> "How do we know but that in that mystical legislation . . . there may not be a law of limitations by which the debts overdue through time are the same as forgiven? . . . It may be the complicity of all mortal beings is such that the pain he inflicted was endured to his behoof, and that it has helped him atone for his sins as an acceptable offering in the sort of vicarious atonement which has always been in the world."[20]

And why may that paradox not also tell one of the secrets of the Black Cross?

Atonement may explain why the Black Cross was nailed "Aslant from left to right." It slants because someone is bearing it, a Christian idea[21] essential to the background of the friend's interpretation, though the narrator, like a true agnostic, hastens away from directly Christian implications. A careful reader of "Black Cross Farm" soon notes that the poem lacks an ingredient essential to realism. "The King Dines" or "Materials of a Story," like *The Mother and the Father* or "Captain Dunlevy's Last Trip," paint sharp portraits of character, as the writing of many novels had taught Howells to do. In those poems deep, particularized compassion matches the portraiture: the poetry registers (or we readers register) each character's pain acutely. In "Black Cross Farm," however, the *donné* of the poem bars us from access to personal pain. The cryptic message of the Cross speaks for Everyman. Poem and reader register the compassion, the emotion of human solidarity. We are all in this together. Everyone must deny herself, himself, and take up the Black Cross of human woe.

The same general point registers itself from the style. "Black Cross Farm," with its variations upon travel writing styles, relaxed yet ironic, or personal essay styles, expresses anything but the swift-moving parsimony of Howells's fiction, farces, or, indeed, other poems. Consider "Monochromes II" called "Living":

How passionately I will my life away
Which I would give all that I have to stay;
How wildly I hurry, for the change I crave,
To hurl myself into the changeless grave!

Unlike most of his poems, "Black Cross Farm" seems not to concentrate on an exact effect. It aims at effects too broad for precision. It has a general, humanistic end in view. Whoever built and painted the Cross and nailed it across the doors of the hay-mow had a message larger than that intended by Robinson's Reuben Bright who, when his wife died, tore down his slaughter-house. Or if the Cross-maker once had a special intention, his motive has been lost in the general decay of the past. In either case, the motive of the poem is human solidarity in the riddle of the painful earth. In its difficult multiplicity, paradox and indeterminacy, its alienation from the past and lostness in the present, its disregard of the mainstream, its faithlessness and despair, its devotion to riddles and dismay, and even in its technique, "Black Cross Farm" is modern.

VI

Within these late Howells poems nothing is more pervasive than tough-minded irony. It speaks from the first poem, "The King Dines," through the last, "The Passengers of a Retarded Submersible," disappearing only from the tributes to "Contemporaries." It needs no display to recall that nothing more characterizes the arts of modernism than irony. Some of these poems deal in perennial themes: death, fate, loss, sorrow and guilt, the tragic sense of life. The treatment is never single, seldom direct. Angles of approach or resolution are plural, often surprisingly, even shockingly oblique. Many of the best and least generally known deal in themes and obliquities one can only call modernist. One sort treats of matters psychological sometimes even to the extreme of spiritualism. Among them stand "Twelve P.M.," the three "Father and Mother" dialogues, "Experience," "The Face at the Window," and "The Passengers of a Retarded Submersible." Another sort is the kind of poem that interested Robinson, Frost, Stevens, and Jeffers. It might be called Americana as objective correlatives for the human condition. I think of "Breakfast Is My Best Meal," "City and Country in the Fall," "Black Cross Farm," and "Captain Dunlevy's Last Trip." And finally there come the often extraordinary poems of social justice: "The King Dines," "Labor and Capital," "Vision," "Society," and "Materials of a Story."

Though these are distinguished for other virtues, too, their modernist power arises from irony. Biographically the springs of Howells's irony welled from many sources. But the irony of this poetry took its rise from certain varieties of religious experience. His anguish over Winifred's death stirred the magic well of his preconscious and creative mind to the lees. Intellectually, however, that experience conflicted with inveterate agnostic denial. Perhaps Howells explained matters best to Howard Pyle, a "mystical" and tender-minded Swedenborgian. With typical self-deprecation, he said to Pyle, "I tell you honestly that for the better part of the time I believe in nothing, though I am afraid of everything. . . . I have had [dreams] about my daughter, fantastic and hideous, as though to punish me for my unbelief." He snubbed Pyle, however, about the question of miracles: "Christ is easy to believe in; he is here and has always been here in our hearts, but did he commit those outlawries, those violations of the order of nature?"[22] Such conflict resolved in irony, especially a self-

XLIII

mockery which converted itself into poetic impulse. And so the poetry spoke of matters that were both religious and not so, and the energy released by conflict lent emotional intensity to the poetry. Such a condition was and is modern.

There were quite naturally other ironies in the contemporary response to this poetry. William Stanley Beaumont Braithwaite, the famous African-American poet, novelist, and anthologist who also served as literary editor of the *Boston Evening Transcript,* reviewed *The Daughter of the Storage* on July 1, 1916. He said that "'The Face at the Window' is as contemporaneous as Frost." He opined that Howells had lost none of "the freshness and vitality of his genius" but "remains the unassailable and incomparable figure in our literature today." Hamilton Wright Mabie, however, took an equivocal view.[23] He had never approved of the modernist trend in Howells. Of *The Rise of Silas Lapham* when it was new he had said that, however masterly, it was a moral failure, even antisocial, because its author was not "loyal" to the romantic vision of "the Whole, the Good, and the True." A realistic and agnostic, Howells, he said, had no imagination, was a cold, poisonous destroyer of passion, hope, and faith.

By long labor in the vineyard of *The Christian Union* and by volumes like *Books and Culture* and *The Life of the Spirit* Mabie ascended to the (Boston) Institute of Arts and Letters, quite unready to think there was any virtue in modernism. And in 1915 it became his duty to present the gold medal of his institute to Howells. In his presentation speech he managed both to shuffle superbly and to pay a compliment intended to be wounding but now laudatory in spite of intent. "A man of the modern temper," Mabie said, "undismayed by the newest method and the latest radicalism, Mr. Howells is always the artist. However advanced his doctrine, his speech never misses the charm which has made art the universal." As Mabie did not expect, he was borne out by a body of poetry he did not know.

NOTES

1. On modernism see Richard Ellman and Charles Feidelson, *The Modern Tradition: Backgrounds of Modern Literature* (New York, 1965). More recently James W. Tuttleton has said concerning "Modernism": "At present the task of definition seems beyond us" ("The Vexations of Modernism: Edmund Wilson's *Axel's Castle*," *The American Scholar* 57 [1988]: 263). Obviously, no single definition is going to end the debate in the near future.

2. Quoted from "A Calendar of the Letters of William Dean Howells," edited by William M. Gibson, George Arms, and F. C. Marston, Jr. Unpublished.

3. Marrion Wilcox, "Works of William Dean Howells," *Harper's Weekly,* July 4, 1898.

4. *William Dean Howells, A Study* (Cambridge, 1924), 254–59, 332.

5. "Mr. Howells as Poet," *Bookman* 2 (February 1896): 525.

6. Mildred Howells, ed., *The Life in Letters of William Dean Howells* (New York, 1928) [hereafter *Life*], 1:425.

7. This thrice-told tale was first told in Cady, *The Realist at War: The Mature Years 1865–1920 of William Dean Howells* (Syracuse, 1958), esp. 56–91. Relevant evidence is presented in *W. D. Howells, Selected Letters* (hereafter *SL*), Vol. 3: 1882–1891, ed. Robert C. Leitz III and others (Boston, 1980), *passim*. The essential evidence has not changed over the past forty years. It is now clear that Weir Mitchell's medical records do not survive.

8. *SL,* 3:247, 248.

9. *SL,* 5:90.

10. *SL,* 3:265, 281, 287.

11. *Life,* 2:57.

12. See Marjorie Louise Henry, *Stuart Merrill: Le contribution d'un Américain au Symbolisme Français* (Paris, 1927), 89 *et passim*.

13. *SL,* 3:295. A full estimate of the significance of Howells's pioneering review may be found in Willis J. Buckingham, ed., *Emily Dickinson's Reception in the 1890s: A Documentary History* (Pittsburgh, 1989), xi–xxiii. For the review in full see Cady, *Howells as Critic,* 189–95.

14. John D. Barry, "A Note on Stephen Crane," *Bookman* (April 1901); see also Joseph Katz, *The Complete Poems of Stephen Crane* (Ithaca, 1972), xiii–xiv *et passim.* The standard source is Daniel Hoffman, *The Poetry of Stephen Crane* (New York, 1957).

15. *SL,* 4:213.

16. *SL,* 4:68.

17. *Life,* 2:34–35.

18. "The Editor's Easy Chair," *Harper's Monthly* 131 (September 1915): 634.

19. *Selected Letters of Robert Frost,* ed. Lawrence Thompson (New York, 1954), 265.

20. *The Son of Royal Langbrith* (New York, 1905), 369.

21. See Mark 8:34, Matthew 10:38, and Luke 9:23, 14:27.

22. *Life,* 2:11, 61

23. Hamilton Wright Mabie, "A Typical Novel," *Andover Review* 4 (November 1885): 417–20. Mabie's presentation speech is quoted in Clara M. Kirk, *W. D. Howells and Art in His Time* (New Brunswick, N.J., 1964), 264.

IMPRESSIONS

Impression
Two people on a bench in Boston Common,
An ordinary laboring man and woman,
Seated together,
In the November weather
Slit with a thin, keen rain;
The woman's mouth purple with cold and pain,
And her eyes fixed as if they did not see
The passers trooping by continually,
Smearing the elm leaves underfoot that fall
Before her on the miry mall;
The man feeding out of the newspaper
Wrapped round the broken victuals brought with her,
And gnawing at a bent bone like a dog,
Following its curve hungrily with his teeth,
And his head twisted sidewise; and beneath
His reeking boots the mud, and the gray fog
Fathomless over him, and all the gloom
Of the day round him for his dining-room.

NOVEMBER. — IMPRESSION.

A weft of leafless spray
Woven fine against the gray
Of the autumnal day,
And blurred along those ghostly garden tops
Clusters of berries crimson as the drops
That my heart bleeds when I remember
How often, in how many a far November,
Of childhood and my children's childhood I was glad,
With the wild rapture of the Fall
Thrilling from me to them, of all
The ruin now so intolerably sad.

Impression

A spiteful snow spit through the bitter day
In little stinging pellets gray,
And crackling on the frozen street
About the iron feet,
Broad stamped in massy shoes
Sharpened and corked for winter use,
Of the huge Norman horses plump and round,
In burnished brass and shining leather bound,
Dragging each heavy fetlock like a mane,
And shaking as they pull the ponderous wain
With wheels that jar the ground
In a small earthquake, where they jolt and grind,
And leave a span-wide track behind:
And hunched upon the load
Above the Company's horses like a toad,
All hugged together
Against the pitiless weather,
In an old cardigan jacket and a cap
Of mangy fur,
And a frayed comforter
Around his stiffened chin, too scant to wrap
His purple ears,
And in his blinking eyes what had been tears,
But that they seemed to have frozen there ere they ran,
The Company's man.

MOODS

I. ANOTHER DAY

Another day, and with it that brute joy,
Or that prophetic rapture of the boy
Whom every morning brings as glad a breath
As if it dawned upon the end of death!

All other days have run the common course,
And left me at their going neither worse
Nor better for them; only, a little older,
A little sadder, and a little colder.

But this, it seems as if this day might be
The day I somehow always thought to see,
And that should come to bless me past the scope
And measure of my farthest-reaching hope.

To-day, maybe, the things that were concealed
Before the first day was, shall be revealed,
The riddle of our misery shall be read,
And it be clear whether the dead are dead.

Before this sun shall sink into the west
The tired earth may have fallen on his breast,
And into heaven the world have passed away . . .
At any rate, it is another day!

II. LIFE

Once a thronged thoroughfare that wound afar
By shining streams, and waving fields and woods,
And festal cities and sweet solitudes,
All whither, onward to the utmost star:

Now a blind alley, lurking by the shore
Of stagnant ditches, walled with reeking crags,
Where one old heavy-hearted vagrant lags,
Footsore, at nightfall limping to Death's door.

III. TEMPERAMENT

Where love and hate, honor and infamy,
Change and dissolve away, and cease to be;
Where good and evil in effect are one
In the long tale of years beneath the sun;
Where like the face a man sees in a glass
And turns from, character itself shall pass—
Out of the mystery whence we came we bring
One thing that is the one immutable thing,
Through which we fashion all that we do here,
Which is the body of our hope and fear,
The form of all we feel and all we know,
The color of our weal and of our woe,
And which alone, it may be, we shall bear
Back to that mystery when we go there.

IV. WEATHER-BREEDER

Ah, not to know that such a happiness
To be wished greater were to be made less;
That one drop more must make it spill in tears
Of agony that blisters and that sears;
That the supreme perfection of thy bliss
Alone could mother misery like this!

V. PEONAGE

How tired the Recording Angel must begin
To be of setting down the same old sin,
The same old folly, year out and year in,
Since I knew how to err, against my name!
It makes me sick at heart and sore with shame
To think of that monotony of blame
For things I fancied once that I should be
Quits with in doing; but at last I see
All that I did became a part of me,
And cannot be put from me, but must still
Remain a potent will within my will,
Holding me debtor, while I live, to ill.

VI. SOME ONE ELSE

Live my life over? I would rather not.
Though I could choose, perhaps, a fairer lot,
I cannot hope I should be worthier it,
Or wiser by experience any whit.
Being what I am, I should but do once more
The things that brought me grief and shame before.
But I should really fancy trying again
For some one else who had lived once in vain:
Somehow another's erring life allures;
And were I you, I might improve on yours.

MONOCHROMES

I. QUESTION

Shall it be after the long misery
   Of easeless pillows, and the waste of flesh
   In sickness, till some worn and widening mesh
Frays out at last, and lets the soul go free?
Or, shall some violent accident suddenly
   Dismiss it, or some black cloud in the brain
   Lower till life maddens against life amain?
Where, in what land, or on what lonely sea?
   When, in the light of what unrisen sun?
   Under what fatal planet? There is none
Can tell, or know aught but that it shall be:
   The one thing certain which all other things
   Have taught my being in its inmost springs
To feel the sole impossibility.

II. LIVING

How passionately I will my life away
Which I would give all that I have to stay;
How wildly I hurry, for the change I crave,
To hurl myself into the changeless grave!

III. COMPANY

I thought, "How terrible, if I were seen
Just as in will and deed I have always been!
And if this were the fate that I must face
At the last day, and all else were God's grace,
How must I shrink and cower before them there,
Stripped naked to the soul and beggared bare
Of every rag of seeming!" Then, "Why, no,"
I thought, "why should I, if the rest are so?"

IV. TO-MORROW

Old fraud, I know you in that gay disguise,
That air of hope, that promise of surprise:
Beneath your bravery, as you come this way,
I see the sordid presence of To-day;
And I shall see there, long ere you are gone,
All the dull Yesterdays that I have known.

V. FRIENDS AND FOES

Bitter the things one's enemies will say
Against one sometimes when one is away,
But of a bitterness far more intense
The things one's friends will say in one's defence.

VI. FROM GENERATION TO GENERATION

I

Innocent spirits, bright, immaculate ghosts!
Why throng your heavenly hosts,
As eager for their birth
In this sad home of death, this sorrow-haunted earth?
Beware! Beware! Content you where you are,
And shun this evil star,
Where we who are doomed to die,
Have our brief being and pass, we know not where or why.

II

We have not to consent or to refuse;
It is not ours to choose:
We come because we must,
We know not by what law, if unjust or if just.

The doom is on us, as it is on you,
That nothing can undo;
And all in vain you warn:
As your fate is to die, our fate is to be born.

VII. THE BEWILDERED GUEST

I was not asked if I should like to come.
   I have not seen my host here since I came,
   Or had a word of welcome in his name.
Some say that we shall never see him, and some
That we shall see him elsewhere, and then know
   Why we were bid. How long I am to stay
   I have not the least notion. None, they say,
Was ever told when he should come or go.
But every now and then there bursts upon
   The song and mirth a lamentable noise,
   A sound of shrieks and sobs, that strikes our joys
Dumb in our breasts; and then, some one is gone.
They say we meet him. None knows where or
      when.
We know we shall not meet him here again.

VIII. IF

Yes, death is at the bottom of the cup,
And every one that lives must drink it up;
And yet between the sparkle at the top
And the black lees where lurks that bitter drop,
There swims enough good liquor, Heaven knows,
To ease our hearts of all their other woes.

The bubbles rise in sunshine at the brim;
That drop below is very far and dim;
The quick fumes spread and shape us such bright dreams
That in the glad delirium it seems
As though by some deft sleight, if so we willed,
That drop untasted might be somehow spilled.

IX. RESPITE

Drowsing, the other afternoon, I lay
   In that sweet interlude that falls between
   Waking and sleeping, when all being is seen
Of one complexion, and the vague dreams play
Among the thoughts, and the thoughts go astray
   Among the dreams. My mother, who has been
   Dead almost half my life, appeared to lean
Above me, a boy, in a house far away,
That once was home, and all the troubled years
   That have been since were as if they were not.
The voices that are hushed were in my ears,
   The looks and motions that I had forgot
Were in my eyes; and they disowned the tears
   That now again beneath their lids are hot.

STOPS OF VARIOUS QUILLS

I. SPHINX

We who are nothing but self, and have no manner of being
   Save in the sense of self, still have no other delight
Like the relief that comes with the blessed oblivion freeing
   Self from self in the deep sleep of some dreamless night.

Losing alone is finding; the best of being is ceasing
   Now and again to be. Then at the end of this strife,
That which comes, if we will it or not, for our releasing,
   Is it eternal death, or is it infinite life?

II. TWELVE P.M.

To get home from some scene of gayety,
   Say a long dinner, and the laugh and joke,
   And funny story, and tobacco smoke,
   And all the not unkindly fatuousness
   Of fellow-beings not better and not worse
   Than others are, but gorged with course on course,
   And drenched with wine; and with one's evening dress
To take off one's perfunctory smile, and be
   Wholly and solely one's sheer self again—
   Is like escaping from some dull, dumb pain;
   And in the luxury of that relief,
   It is, in certain sort and measure, as if
   One had put off the body, and the whole
   Illusion of life, and in one's naked soul
Confronted the eternal Verity.

III. TIME

Do you wish me, then, away?
You should rather bid me stay:
Though I seem so dull and slow,
Think before you let me go!

Whether you entreat or spurn
I can nevermore return:
Times shall come, and times shall be,
But no other time like me.

Though I move with leaden feet,
Light itself is not so fleet;
And before you know me gone
Eternity and I are one.

IV. GOOD SOCIETY

Yes, I suppose it is well to make some sort of exclusion,
    Well to put up the bars, under whatever pretence;
Only be careful, be very careful, lest in the confusion
    You should shut yourself on the wrong side of the fence.

V. HEREDITY

That swollen paunch you are doomed to bear
Your gluttonous grandsire used to wear;
That tongue, at once so light and dull,
Wagged in your grandam's empty skull;
The leering of the sensual eye
Your father, when he came to die,
Left yours alone; and that cheap flirt,
Your mother, gave you from the dirt
The simper which she used upon
So many men ere he was won.

Your vanity and greed and lust
Are each your portion from the dust
Of those that died, and from the tomb
Made you what you must needs become.
I do not hold you aught to blame
For sin at second hand, and shame:
Evil could but from evil spring;
And yet, away, you charnel thing!

VI. IN THE DARK

How often, when I wake from sleep at night,
    I search my consciousness to find the ill
    That has lurked formlessly within it, still
Haunting me with a shadowy affright;
And try to seize it and to know aright
    Its vague proportions, and my frantic will
    Runs this way and runs that way, with a thrill
Of horror, to all things that ban or blight!
Then, when I find all well, it is as though
    The moment were some reef where I had crept
    From the wide waste of danger and of death,
    And for a little I might draw my breath
    Before the flood came up again, and swept
Over it, and gulfed me in its deeps below.

VII. SOLITUDE

Ah, you cannot befriend me, with all your love's tender
    persistence!
In your arms' pitying clasp sole and remote I remain,
Rapt as far from help as the last star's measureless distance,
    Under the spell of our life's innermost mystery, Pain.

VIII. CHANGE

Sometimes, when after spirited debate
   Of letters or affairs, in thought I go
   Smiling unto myself, and all aglow
With some immediate purpose, and elate
As if my little, trivial scheme were great,
   And what I would so were already so:
   Suddenly I think of her that died, and know,
Whatever friendly or unfriendly fate
   Befall me in my hope or in my pride,
It is all nothing but a mockery,
And nothing can be what it used to be,
   When I could bid my happy life abide,
And build on earth for perpetuity,
   Then, in the deathless days before she died.

IX. MIDWAY

So blithe the birds sang in the trees,
    The trees sang in the wind,
I winged me with the morning breeze,
    And left Care far behind.

But now both birds and trees are mute
    In the hot hush of noon;
And I must up and on afoot,
    Or Care will catch me soon.

X. CONSCIENCE

Judge me not as I judge myself, O Lord!
    Show me some mercy, or I may not live:
Let the good in me go without reward;
    Forgive the evil I must not forgive!

XI. CALVARY

If He could doubt on His triumphant cross,
How much more I, in the defeat and loss
Of seeing all my selfish dreams fulfilled,
Of having lived the very life I willed,
Of being all that I desired to be?
My God, my God! Why hast thou forsaken me?

PEBBLES

THE BURDEN

I writhed beneath my burden, fumed and groaned.
My burden that had felt and heard me, moaned:
"You do not know what misery is, nor what
The bitterest part is of our common lot.
The strength I load in you with my loath weight,
My weakness would so gladly own its fate.
Think, once, how much more dreadful it must be
To be the burden than bear it, and pity me!"

HOPE

We sailed and sailed upon the desert sea
Where for whole days we alone seemed to be.
At last we saw a dim, vague line arise
Between the empty billows and the skies,
That grew and grew until it wore the shape
Of cove and inlet, promontory and cape;
Then hills and valleys, rivers, fields, and woods,
Steeples and roofs, and village neighborhoods.
And then I thought, "Sometime I shall embark
Upon a sea more desert and more dark
Than ever this was, and between the skies
And empty billows I shall see arise
Another world out of that waste and lapse,
Like yonder land. Perhaps—perhaps—perhaps!"

SYMPATHY

Friend, neighbor, stranger, as the case may be,
You who are sitting in the stall next to me,
And listening also to this pitiless play
That says for me all that I would not say,
And follows me, however I wind about,
And seems to turn my whole life inside out:
I wonder, should I speak and be the first
To own just where in my soul it hurt worst,
And you revealed in yours the spot its flame
Scorched fiercest, if it might not be the same.

VISION

Within a poor man's squalid home I stood:
    The one bare chamber, where his work-worn wife
    Above the stove and wash-tub passed her life,
Next the sty where they slept with all their brood.

But I saw not that sunless, breathless lair,
    The chamber's sagging roof and reeking floor;
    The smeared walls, broken sash, and battered door;
The foulness and forlornness everywhere.

I saw a great house with the portals wide
    Upon a banquet room, and, from without,
    The guests descending in a brilliant line
By the stair's statued niches, and beside
    The loveliest of the gemmed and silken rout
    The poor man's landlord leading down to dine.

REWARD AND PUNISHMENT

You are the best and the worst of everything you require.
  If you have looked on shame willingly, yours is the shame.
You are the evil you mean, and you are the good you desire;
  You shall be for yourself both the praise and the blame.

PARABLE

The young man who had great possessions dreamed
That once again he came to Christ and seemed
To hear Him making answer as before,
"Sell all thou hast and give unto the poor,
And come and follow me." And now he did
In all immediately as Jesus bid.

Then some of them to whom he gave his wealth
Mocked at him for a fool or mad, by stealth
Or openly; and others he could see
Wasting his substance with a spendthrift glee;

And others yet were tempted, and drawn in
The ways of sin that had not dreamed of sin:
Others, besides, that took were robbed and killed:
Some that had toiled their whole lives were unwilled
By riches, and began the life accurst
Of idleness, like rich men from the first.
Some hid his money in the earth, a root
From which should grow a flower of deadly fruit;
Some kept, and put it out at usury,
And made men slaves with it that had been free.

The young man's dream was broken with his grief,
And he awoke to his immense relief,
And wept for joy, and cried, "He could not know
What dire results from His behest would flow!
I must not follow Him, but I can fulfil
The spirit, if not the letter, of His will.

Seeing the things I have been shown in sleep,
I realize how much better 'twere to keep
The means that Providence has bestowed on me,
Doubtless for some wise purpose, and to be
The humble agency and instrument
Of good to others not intelligent
Enough to use the gifts of God aright."
He rose up with a heart at peace, and light;
And thenceforth none of the Deserving Poor
Ever went empty-handed from his door.

STATISTICS

So many men, on such a date of May,
Despaired and took their hopeless lives away
In such an area, year after year;
In such another place, it would appear
The assassinations averaged so and so,
Through August after August, scarce below
A given range; and in another one,
March after March, it seems there were undone
So many women still about the same,
With little varying circumstance in their shame;
Burglaries, arsons, thefts, and forgeries
Had their own averages as well as these;
And from these figures science can discern
The future in the past. We but return
Upon our steps, although they seem so free.
The thing that has been is that which shall be.

Dark prophet, yes! But still somehow the round
Is spiral, and the race's feet have found
The path rise under them which they have trod.
Your facts are facts, yet somewhere there is God.

POEMS, 1891–1895

WHAT SHALL IT PROFIT?

If I lay waste and wither up with doubt
The blessed fields of heaven where once my faith
Possessed itself serenely safe from death;
If I deny the things past finding out;
Or if I orphan my own soul of One
That seemed a Father, and make void the place
Within me where He dwelt in power and grace,
What do I gain by that I have undone?

MORTALITY

How many times have I lain down at night,
And longed to fall into that gulf of sleep
Whose dreamless deep
Is haunted by no memory of
The weary world above;
And thought myself most miserable that I
Must impotently lie
So long upon the brink
Without the power to sink
Into that nothingness, and neither feel nor think!

How many times, when day brought back the light
After the merciful oblivion
Of such unbroken slumber,
And once again began to cumber
My soul with her forgotten cares and sorrows,
And show in long perspective the gray morrows,
Stretching monotonously on,
Forever narrowing but never done,
Have I not loathed to live again and said,
It would have been far better to be dead,
And yet somehow, I know not why,
Remained afraid to die!

The Wit supreme, and sovereign Sage,
Has told us all the world's a stage;
The curtain on his scene up-furled
Shows us the stage is all the world.

JUDGMENT DAY

Before Him weltered like a shoreless sea
The souls of them that had not sought to be,
With all their guilt upon them, and they cried,
They that had sinned from hate and lust and pride,
"Thou that didst make us what we might become,
Judge us!" The Judge of all the earth was dumb;
But high above them, in His sovereign place,
He lifted up the pity of His face.

"EXCEPT AS LITTLE CHILDREN"

Lost selves of us poor men and women grown,
　The little children always seem to me:
　Ah, if we could but find them once and be
Lost in them when they come into their own!

RACE

I

    Leave me here those looks of yours!
All those pretty airs and lures;
Flush of cheek and flash of eye;
Your lips' smile and their deep dye;
Gleam of the white teeth within;
Dimple of the cloven chin;
All the sunshine that you wear
In the summer of your hair;
All the morning of your face;
All your figure's wilding grace;
The flower-pose of your head, the light
Flutter of your footsteps' flight:
I own all, and that glad heart
I must claim ere you depart.

II

    Go, yet go not unconsoled!
Sometime, after you are old,
You shall come, and I will take
From your brow the sullen ache,
From your eyes the twilight gaze
Darkening upon winter days,
From your feet their palsy pace,
And the wrinkles from your face,
From your locks the snow; the droop
Of your head, your worn frame's stoop,
And that withered smile within

The kissing of the nose and chin:
I own all, and that sad heart
I will claim ere you depart.

III

    I am Race, and both are mine,
Mortal Age and Youth divine:
Mine to grant, but not in fee;
Both again revert to me
From each that lives, that I may give
Unto each that yet shall live.

SOCIETY

I looked and saw a splendid pageantry
   Of beautiful women and lordly men,
   Taking their pleasure in a flowery plain,
Where poppies and red anemone,
And many another leaf of cramoisy,
   Flickered about their feet, and gave their stain
   To heels of iron or satin, and the grain
Of silken garments floating far and free,
As in the dance they wove themselves, or strayed
   By twos together, or lightly smiled and bowed,
Or curtseyed to each other, or else played
At games of mirth and pastime, unafraid
   In their delight; and all so high and proud
   They seemed scarce of the earth whereupon they trod.

II

I looked again and saw that flowery space
   Stirring, as if alive, beneath the tread
   That rested now upon an old man's head
And now upon a baby's gasping face,
Or mother's bosom, or the rounded grace
   Of a girls' throat; and what had seemed the red
   Of flowers was blood, in gouts and gushes shed
From hearts that broke under that frolic pace.
And now and then from out the dreadful floor
   An arm or brow was lifted from the rest,
As if to strike in madness, or implore

For mercy; and anon some suffering breast
Heaved from the mass and sank; and as before
The revellers above them thronged and prest.

EQUALITY

The beautiful dancing-women wove their maze,
   With many a swift lascivious leer and lure
For the hot theatre, whose myriad gaze
   Burned on their shamelessness with eyes impure.

Then one that watched unseen among them—dread,
Mystical, ineffable of presence—said,
"Patience! And leave me these poor wanton ones:
Soon they shall lie as meek and cold as nuns;
And you that hire them here to tempt your lust
Shall be as all the saints are, in the dust."

SCENE AND STORY

I met a friend of mine the other day
Upon the platform of a West End car;
We shook hands, and my friend began to say
Quickly, as if he were not going far,
"Last summer something rather in your way
Came to my knowledge. I was asked to see
A young man who had come to talk with me
Because I was a clergyman; and he
Told me at once that he had served his time
In the state-prison for a heinous crime,
And was just out. He had no friends, or none
To speak of; and he seemed far gone
With a bad cough. He said he had not done
The thing. They all say that. You cannot tell.
He might not have been guilty of it. Well,
What he now wanted was some place to stay,
And work that he could do. I managed it
With no great trouble. And then, there began
The strangest thing I ever knew. The man,
Who showed no other signs of a weak wit,
Was hardly settled in his place a week
When he came round to see me, and to speak
About his lodging. What the matter was
He could not say, or would not tell the cause,
But he must leave that place; he could not bear
To stay. I found another room, but there
After another week he could not stay.

Again I placed him, and he came to say
At the week's end that he must go away.
So it went on, week after week, and then
At last I made him tell me. It appears
That his imprisonment of fifteen years
Had worn so deep into the wretch's brain
That any place he happened to remain
Longer than one day in began to seem
His prison and all over again to him;
And when the thing had got into this shape,
He was quite frantic till he could escape.
Curious, was not it? And tragical."
"Tragical? I believe you! Was that all?
What has become of him?" "Oh, he is dead.
I told some people of him, and we made
A decent funeral for him. At the end
It came out that his mother was alive—
An outcast—and she asked our leave to attend
The ceremony, and then asked us to give
The silver coffin plate, carved with his name,
And the flowers, to her." "That was touching. She
Had some good left her in her infamy."
"Why, I don't know! I think she sold the things,
Together with a neck-pin and some rings
That he had left, and drank. . . . But as to blame. . . .
Good-morning to you!" and my friend stepped down
At the street crossing. I went on up town.

BREAKFAST IS MY BEST MEAL

Overheard at Carlsbad

I

Breakfast is my best meal, and I reckon it's always been
Ever since I was old enough to know what breakfast could mean.
I mind when we lived in the cabin out on the Illinoy,
Where father had took up a quarter-section when I was a boy,
I used to go for the cows as soon as it was light;
And when I started back home, before I come in sight,
I come in *smell* of the cabin, where mother was frying the ham,
And boiling the coffee, that reached through the air like a mile o'
    ba'm,
'N' I bet you I didn't wait to see what it was that the dog
Thought he'd got under the stump or inside o' the hollow log!
But I made the old cows canter till their hoofjoints cracked—you
    know
That dry, funny kind of a noise that the cows make when they go—
And I never stopped to wash when I got to the cabin door;
I pulled up my chair and e't like I never had e't before.
And mother she set there and watched me eat, and eat, and eat,
Like as if she couldn't give her old eyes enough of the treat;
And she split the shortened biscuit, and spread the butter between,
And let it lay there and melt, and soak and soak itself in;
And she piled up my plate with potato and ham and eggs,
Till I couldn't hold any more, or hardly stand on my legs;
And she filled me up with coffee that would float an iron wedge,
And never give way a mite, or spill a drop at the edge.

II

What? Well, yes, this is good coffee, too. If they don't know much,
They do know how to make coffee, I *will* say that for these Dutch.
But my—oh, my! It ain't the kind of coffee my mother made,
And the coffee my wife used to make would throw it clear in the
    shade;
And the brand of sugar-cured, canvased ham that she always used—
Well, this Westphalia stuff would simply have made her amused!
That so, heigh? I saw that you was United States as soon
As ever I heard you talk; I reckon I know the tune!
Pick it out anywhere; and *you* understand how I feel
About these here foreign breakfasts: breakfast is my best meal.

III

My! but my wife was a cook; and the breakfasts she used to get
The first years we was married, I can smell 'em and taste 'em yet:
Corn cake light as a feather, and buckwheat thin as lace
And crisp as cracklin'; and steak that you couldn't have the face
To compare any steak over here to; and chicken fried
Maryland style—I couldn't get through the bill if I tried.
And then, her waffles! My! She'd kind of slip in a few
Between the ham and the chicken—you know how women'll do—
For a sort of little surprise, and, if I was running light,
To take my fancy and give an edge to my appetite.
Done it all herself as long as we was poor, and I tell *you*
She liked to see me eat as well as mother used to do;
I reckon she went ahead of mother some, if the truth was known,
And everything she touched she give a taste of her own.

IV

She was a cook, I can tell you! And after we got ahead,
And she could 'a' had a girl to do the cookin' instead,
I had the greatest time to get Momma to leave the work;
She said it made her feel like a mis'able sneak and shirk.
She didn't want daughter, though, when we did begin to keep girls,
To come in the kitchen and cook, and smell up her clo'es and curls;
But you couldn't have stopped the child, whatever you tried to do—
I reckon the gift of the cookin' was born in Girly, too.
Cook she would from the first, and we just had to let her alone;
And after she got married, and had a house of her own,
She tried to make me feel, when I come to live with her,
Like it was my house, too; and I tell you she done it, sir!
She remembered that breakfast was my best meal, and she tried
To have all I used to have, and a good deal more beside;
Grape-fruit to begin with, or melons or peaches, at least—
Husband's business took him there, and they had went to live East—
Then a Spanish macker'l, or a soft-shell crab on toast,
Or a broiled live lobster! Well, sir, I don't want to seem to boast,
But I don't believe you could have got in the whole of New York
Any such an oyster fry or sausage of country pork.

V

Well, I don't know what-all it means; I alway lived just so—
Never drinked or smoked, and yet, here about two years ago,
I begun to run down; I ain't as young as I used to be;
And the doctors all said Carlsbad, and I reckon this is me.
But it's more like some one I've dreamt of, with all three of 'em gone!

69

Believe in ghosts? Well, *I* do. I *know* there are ghosts. I'm *one.*
Maybe I mayn't look it—I was always inclined to fat;
The doctors say that's the trouble, and very likely it's that.
This is my little grandson, and this is the oldest one
Of Girly's girls; and for all that the whole of us said and done,
She must come with grandpa when the doctors sent me off here,
To see that they didn't starve him. Ain't that about so, my dear?
She can cook, I tell you; and when we get home again
We're goin' to have something to *eat;* I'm just a-livin' till then.
But when I set here of a morning, and think of them that's gone—
Mother and Momma and Girly—well, I wouldn't like to let on
Before the children, but I can almost seem to see
All of 'em lookin' down, like as if they pitied me,
After the breakfasts they give me, to have me have to put up
With nothing but bread and butter, and a little mis'able cup
Of this here weak-kneed coffee! I can't tell how *you* feel,
But it fairly makes me sick! Breakfast is my best meal.

FATHER AND MOTHER: A MYSTERY

The parlor of a village house, with open doors and windows; the Father and the Mother sitting alone among the chairs in broken rows; a piano with a lifted lid; dust tracked about the floor.

The Father: "Now it is over."

The Mother: "It is over, now,
And we shall never see her any more."

The Father: "Have you put everything of hers away?
If I found anything that she had worn,
Or that had belonged to her, I think the sight
Would kill me."

The Mother: "Oh, you need not be afraid;
I have put everything away."

The Father: "Oh, me!
How shall we do without her! It is as if
One of my arms had been lopped off, and I
Must go through life a mutilated man.
This morning when I woke there was an instant,
A little instant, when she seemed alive,
Before the clouds closed over me again,
And death filled all the world. Then came that stress,
That horrible impatience to be done
With what had been our child. As if to hide
The cold white witness of her absence were
To have her back once more!"

The Mother: "I felt that, too.
I thought I could not rest till it was done;

71

And now I cannot rest, and we shall rest
Never again as long as we shall live.
Our grief will drug us, yes, and we shall sleep,
As we have slept already; but not rest."
    The Father: "We must, I cannot help believing it,
See her again some time and somewhere else."
    The Mother: "Oh, never, any time or anywhere!"
    The Father: "You used to think we should."
    The Mother: "I know I did.
But that is gone forever, that fond lie
With which we used to fool our happiness,
When we had no need of it. When we had
Each other safe we could not even imagine
Not having one another always."
    The Father: "Yes,
It was a lie, a cruel, mocking lie!"
    The Mother: "Why did you ask me, then? Do you
    suppose
That if the love we used to make believe
Would reunite is, really had the power,
It would not, here and now, be doing it,
Now, when we need her more than we shall need her
Even in all eternity, and she—
If she is still alive, which I deny—
Is aching for us both as we for her?
You know how much she loved her home, and how
She suffered if she left it for a week;
You know how lost and heart-sick she must be,

Wherever she is, if she is anywhere;
And if her longing and if ours could bring us
Together as we used to dream it could,
How soon she would be here!"
    The Father: "I cannot bear it!"
    The Mother: "I shall not care, when you and I are old,
Years hence, and we shall have begun to be
Forgetful, as old people are, about her,
And all her looks and ways—I shall not care
To see her then. I want to see her now,
Now while I still remember everything,
And she remembers, and has all her faults,
Just as we have our own, to be forgiven.
But if we have to wait till she is grown
Some frigid, perfect angel, in some world
Where she has other ties, I shall not care
To see her; I should be afraid of her."
    The Father: "She would not then be she, nor we be we."
    The Mother: "I want to tell her how I grieve for all
I ever did or said that was unkind
Since she was born. But if we met above,
In that impossible heaven, she would not care."
    The Father: "If she knows anything she knows that now
Without your telling."
    The Mother: "I want *her* to say
She knows it."
    The Father: "Yet, somehow she seems alive.
The whole way home she seemed to be returning

73

Between us, as she used when we came home
From walking and she was a child."
   The Mother: "Oh, that
Was nothing but the habit of her: just
As if you really had lost an arm
You would have felt it there."
   The Father: "Oh, yes, I know.
          [He lets his head hang in silence; then he looks up at the
                    window opening on the porch.
This honeysuckle's sweetness sickens me.
                   [He rises and shuts the window.
I never shall smell that sweetness while I live
And not die back into this day of death.
                   [He remains at the window
                       staring out.

How still it is outside! The timothy
Stands like a solid wall beside the swath
The men have cut. The clover heads hang heavy
And motionless."
   The Mother: "I wish that it would rain,
And lay the dust. The house is full of dust
From the road yonder. They have tracked it in
Through all the rooms, and I shall have enough
To do getting it out again."
   The Father: "The sun
Pours down its heat as if it were raining fire.
But she that used to suffer so with cold,
She cannot feel it. Did you see that woman,

That horrible old woman, chewing dill
All through the services?"
The Mother: "Oh, yes, I saw her.
You know her: Mrs. Jayne, that always comes
To funerals."
The Father: "I remember. She should be
Prevented, somehow."
The Mother: "Why, she did no harm."
The Father: "I could not bear to have them stand and stare
So long at her dead face. I hate that custom."
The Mother: "I wonder that you cared. It was not *her* face,
Nor the form hers; only a waxen image
Of what she had been. Nothing now is she!
There is no place in the whole universe
For her whose going takes all from the earth
That ever made it home."
The Father: "Yes, she is gone,
And it is worse than if she had not been. . . .
Hark!"
The Mother: "How you startle me! You are so nervous!"
The Father: "I thought I heard a kind of shuddering noise!"
The Mother: "It was a shutter shaking in the wind."
The Father: "There is no wind."
The Mother (after a moment): "Go and see what it was.
It seemed like something in the room where she—"
The Father: "It sounded like the beating of birds' wings.
There! It has stopped."
The Mother: "I must know what it was.

If you will not go, I will. I shall die
Unless you go at once."
  The Father: "Oh, I will go."
  [He goes out and mounts the stairs, which creak under his tread.
   His feet are heard on the floor above. After a moment comes the
         sound of opening and closing shutters.
  The Mother (calling up): "What is it? Quick!"
  The Father (calling down): "It was some kind of bird
Between the shutters and the sash. I cannot
Imagine how it got there."
  [He descends the stairs slowly and comes into the room where the
            Mother sits waiting.
  The Mother: "What bird was it?"
  The Father: "Some kind I did not know. I wish that I
Had let it in."
  The Mother: "What do you mean by that?
Everything living tries to leave the house;
We stay because we are part of death,
And cannot go."
  The Father: "It did not wish to go;
It was not trying to get out, but in.
I put it out once and it came again;
And now I wish that I had let it stay."
  The Mother: "You are so superstitious; and you think. . . ."
      [She stops, and they both sit silent for a time.
  The Father: "It may be our despair that keeps her from us."
  The Mother: "You think, then, that our hope could bring
her to us?"

76

The Father: "Not that, no."

The Mother: "Or, that we could make her live
Again by willing it sufficiently?"

The Father: "Oh no,
Not by our willing; by our loving, yes!
Not through our will, which is a part of us,
And filled full of ourselves, but through our love,
Which is a part of some life else, and filled
With something not ourselves, but better, purer."

The Mother: "Well, try."

The Father: "I cannot. Your doubt palsies me."

The Mother: "I cannot help it. If she cannot come
Unto my doubt, she cannot to my faith. . . .
Oh! What was that?"

The Father: "The wind among the chords
Of the piano. They have left it open
After the singing."

The Mother: "But there is no wind!
You said yourself, just now, there was no wind."

The Father: "Perhaps it was our voices jarred the strings."

The Mother: "They could not do it; and it was not like
Anything that I ever heard before.
It was like something heard within my brain,
And there is something that I see within!
Hark! Look! Do you hear nothing? Do you see
Nothing? Or am I going wild?"

The Father: "No, no!
I hear and see it too. Are you afraid?"

The Mother: "No, not in the least. But, oh, how strange it is!
What is it like to you?"

The Father: "I dare not say,
For fear that it should cease to be at all."

The Mother: "Do you believe that we are dreaming it?
That we are sleeping and are dreaming it?"

The Father: "He could not be so cruel!"

The Mother: "He made death."

The Father: "There! You have hurt it, and it will not speak;
You have offended it. Speak to it!"

The Mother: "Child,
I did not mean to grieve you. Oh, forgive
Your poor old mother! Is she here yet, dearest?"

The Father: "Yes, she is here! Yes, I am sure of it—"

The Mother: "I seemed to have lost her—No, she is here again!
How natural she is! How strong and bright,
And all that sick look gone! It must be true
That it is she, but how shall we be sure
After it passes? Where is it you see her?
Where is it that you hear her speak?"

The Father: "Within.
Within my brain, my heart, my life, my love!"

The Mother: "Yes, that is where I see and hear her too.
And oh, I feel her! This is her dear hand
In mine! How warm and soft it is once more,
After that sickness! Yes, we have her back,
Dearest, we have out child again! But still
How strange it is that she is all within,

And nowhere outside of our minds! Can you
Make her nowhere but in yourself?"

   The Father: "In you—"

   The Mother: "And I in you! I see her in your mind;
I hear her speaking in your mind. That shows
How wholly we are one. Our love has done it,
And we must never quarrel any more.
It was your faith; I will say that for you!
But are you sure we are not dreaming it?"

   The Father: "How could we both be dreaming the same
     thing?"

   The Mother: "We could if we are both so wholly one."

   The Father: "We must not doubt, or it will cease to be.
See! It is growing faint!"

   The Mother: "Oh, no, my child!
I do believe that it is really you.
And, father, you must not keep saying *It*,
As if she were not living. Now she smiles,
And now she is speaking! Can you understand
What she is saying?"

   The Father: "It is not in words,
And yet I understand."

   The Mother: "And so do I.
I wish that you could put it into words
So that we might remember it hereafter."

   The Father: "But what she says cannot be put in words.
It is enough that we can understand
Better than if it were in words."

The Mother: "No, no!
Unless it is in words I am not sure.
Unless she calls you Father and me Mother—
Hush! Did you hear her?"
  The Father: "Yes, I thought I heard her."
  The Mother: "I am sure I heard her call us both, and now
I know it is not a hallucination.
Oh, I believe, and I am satisfied!
But, child, I wish that you could tell me something
About it, where you are! Is it like this?
In everything that I have read about it,
It seemed so vague—"
  The Father: "She answers hesitating,
As we used, when she was a little thing,
To answer her in something that we thought
She would be none the happier for knowing.
Now we are as the children with her, and she is
As father and mother to us, and we must not
Question her."
  The Mother: "Yes. I must; I will, I will!"
  The Father: "There, she is gone! No; she is here again!"
  The Mother: "No; we are somewhere else. What place is
    this?
Is this where she was? Did she bring us here?
It seems as if we now were merged in her
As she was merged in us before *we* came.
But all our wills are one. Oh, mystery!
I am so lost in this strange unity;

Help me to find myself, if you are here!
You *are* here, are you not?"
    The Father: "Yes, I am here,
But not as I was there. I seem a part
Of all that was and is and shall be. This is life,
And that was only living yonder! I can find you,
I can find her, but not myself in it,
Or only as a drop of water may
Find itself in the indiscriminate sea."
    The Mother: "I cannot bear it; I was not prepared!
Oh, save me, dearest! Save me, oh my child!
Speak to me, father, in the words we know,
And not in these intolerable rays
That leave the thought no refuge from itself.
I have not yet the strength to yield my own
Up to this universal happiness.
I still must dwell apart in my own life,
A prison if it need be, or a pang.
Come back with me, both of you, for a while. . . .
Why, I am here again, and you are here!
This is our house, with dust in it and death,
This is dear, dear earthly home! But where is she?
Call to her—tell her we are here again!"
    The Father: "We could not make her come. I am bewildered;
I scarcely know if I am here myself."
    The Mother: "Perhaps she never came at all, and we
Have only dreamed that we were somewhere else.
I feel as if I had awaked from sleep.

How long were we gone?"

The Father: "I cannot tell:
As long as life, or only for an instant."

The Mother: "It could not have been long, for there I see
The humming-bird poised at the honeysuckle
Still, that I noticed when we seemed to go.
Nothing has really happened! yet, somehow. . . .
I wonder what it was she said to us
That satisfied us so? Can you remember?"

The Father: "Not in words, no. It did not seem in words,
And if we tried to put it into words—"

The Mother: "They would be such as mediums use to cheat
Their dupes with, or to make them cheat themselves.
No, no! We ought not to be satisfied.
It is a trick our unstrung nerves have played us.
The selfsame trick has cheated both; or we
Have hypnotized each other. It is the same
As such things have been always from the first:
Our sorrow has made fools of us; we have seen
A phantom that our longing conjured up;
And heard a voice that had no sound; and thought
A meaning into mocking emptiness!"

The Father: "Then, how could it have satisfied us so?"

The Mother: "That was a part of the hallucination.
Nothing has happened, nothing has been proved!"

The Father: "Not to our reason, no, but to our love
Everything."

The Mother: "Then, let her come back again!"

The Father: "Twice would prove nothing more if once

proved nothing.
We have had our glimpse of life beyond the veil;
As every one who sorrows somehow has.
The world is not so hollow as it was.
There still is meaning in the universe;
But if it ever is as waste and senseless
As only now it seemed, and the time comes
When we shall need her as we needed her,
We shall be with her again, or she with us,
Whether the time is somewhere else or here.
Come, mother—mother for eternity!—
Come, let us go, each of us, to our work.
I have been to blame for breaking you with grief
Which I should have supported you against.
Forgive me for it!"
    The Mother: "Oh, what are you saying?
There is no blame, and no forgiveness for it
Between us two, nothing but only love."
    The Father: "The love in which she lives."
    The Mother: "I will believe it.
If you believe it."
    The Father: "Help me to believe!"

CITY AND COUNTRY IN THE FALL

A Long-distance Eclogue

Morrison. Hello! Hello! Is that you, Wetherbee?
Wetherbee. Yes. Who are you? What do you want with me?
Morrison. Oh, nothing much. It's Morrison, you know;
Morrison—down at Clamhurst Shortsands.
    Wetherbee.   Oh!
Why, Morrison, of course! Of course, I know!
How are you, Morrison? And, by the way,
Where are you? What! You never mean to say
You are down there *yet?* Well, by the Holy Poker!
What are you doing there, you ancient joker?
    Morrison. Sticking it out over Thanksgiving Day.
I said I would. I tell you, it is gay
Down here. You ought to see the Hunter's Moon,
These silver nights, prinking in our lagoon.
You ought to see our sunsets, glassy red,
Shading to pink and violet overhead.
You ought to see our mornings, still and clear,
White silence, far as you can look and hear.
You ought to see the leaves—our oaks and ashes
Crimson and yellow, with those gorgeous splashes,
Purple and orange, against the bluish green
Of the pine woods; and scattered in between
The scarlet of the maples; and the blaze
Of blackberry-vines, along the dusty ways
And on the old stone walls; the air just balm,
And the crows cawing through the perfect calm

Of afternoons all gold and turquoise. Say,
You ought to have been with wife and me to-day,
A drive we took—it would have made you sick:
The pigeons and the partridges so thick;
And on the hill just beyond Barkin's lane,
Before you reach the barn of Widow Payne,
Showing right up against the sky, as clear
And motionless as sculpture, stood a deer!
Say, does that jar you just a little? Say,
How have you found things up there, anyway,
Since you got back? Air like a cotton string
To breathe? The same old dust on everything,
And in your teeth, and in your eyes? The smoke
From the soft coal, got long beyond a joke?
The trolleys rather more upon your curves,
And all the roar and clatter in your nerves?
Don't you wish you had stayed here, too?

 Wetherbee.   Well, yes,
I do at certain times, I must confess.
I swear it is enough at times to make you swear
You would almost rather be anywhere
Than here. The building up and pulling down,
The getting to and fro about the town,
The turmoil underfoot and overhead,
Certainly make you wish that you were dead,
At first; and all the mean vulgarity
Of city life, the filth and misery
You see around you, make you want to put
Back to the country anywhere, hot-foot.

Yet—there are compensations.

    Morrison.   Such as?

    Wetherbee.   Why,

There is the club.

    Morrison.   The club I can't deny.

Many o' the fellows back there?

    Wetherbee.   Nearly all.

Over the twilight cocktails there are tall

Stories and talk. But you would hardly care;

You have the natives to talk with down there,

And always find them meaty.

    Morrison.   Well, so-so.

Their words outlast their ideas at times, you know,

And they have *staying* powers. The theaters

All open now?

    Wetherbee.   Yes, all. And it occurs

To me: there's one among the things that you

Would have enjoyed; an opera with the new—

Or at least the last—music by Sullivan,

And words, though not Gilbertian, that ran

Trippingly with it. Oh, I tell you what,

I'd rather that you had been there than not.

    Morrison. Thanks ever so!

    Wetherbee.   Oh, there is nothing mean

About your early friend. That deer and autumn scene

Were kind of you! And, say, I think you like

Afternoon teas when good. I have chanced to strike

Some of the best of late, where people said

They had sent you cards, but thought you must be dead.
I told them I left you down there by the sea,
And then they sort of looked askance at me,
As if it were a joke, and bade me get
Myself some bouillon or some chocolate,
And turned the subject—did not even give
Me time to prove it is not life to live
In town as long as you can keep from freezing
Beside the autumn sea. A little sneezing,
At Clamhurst Shortsands, since the frosts set in?
    Morrison. Well, not enough to make a true friend grin.
Slight colds, mere nothings. With our open fires
We've all the warmth and cheer that heart desires.
Next year we'll have a furnace in, and stay
Not till Thanksgiving, but till Christmas Day.
It's glorious in these roomy autumn nights
To sit between the firelight and the lights
Of our big lamps, and read aloud by turns
As long as kerosene or hickory burns.
We hate to go to bed.
    Wetherbee.   Of course you do!
And hate to get up in the morning, too—
To pull the coverlet from your frost-bit nose,
And touch the glary matting with your toes!
Are you beginning yet to break the ice
In your wash-pitchers? No? Well, that is nice.
I always hate to do it—seems as if
Summer was going; but when your hand is stiff

With cold, it can be done. Still, I prefer
To wash and dress beside my register,
When summer gets a little on, like this.
But some folks find the other thing pure bliss—
Lusty young chaps, like you.
    Morrison.   And some folks find
A sizzling radiator to their mind.
What else have you, there, you could recommend
To the attention of a country friend?
    Wetherbee. Well, you know how it is in Madison
      Square,
Late afternoons, now, if the day's been fair—
How all the western sidewalk ebbs and flows
With pretty women in their pretty clo'es:
I've never seen them prettier than this year.
Of course, I know a dear is not a deer,
But still, I think that if I had to meet
One or the other in the road, or street,
All by myself, I am not sure but that
I'd choose the dear that wears the fetching hat.
    Morrison. Get out! What else?
    Wetherbee.   Well, it is not so bad,
If you are feeling a little down, or sad,
To walk along Fifth Avenue to the Park,
When the day thinks perhaps of getting dark,
And meet that mighty flood of vehicles
Laden with all the different kinds of swells,
Homing to dinner, in their carriages—

Victorias, landaus, chariots, coupés—
There's nothing like it to lift up the heart
And make you realize yourself a part,
Sure, of the greatest show on earth.
    Morrison.   Oh, yes,
I know. I've felt that rapture more or less.
But I would rather put it off as long
As possible. I suppose you like the song
Of the sweet car-gongs better than the cry
Of jays and yellowhammers when the sky
Begins to redden these October mornings,
And the loons sound their melancholy warnings;
Or honk of the wild-geese that write their A
Along the horizon in the evening's gray.
Or when the squirrels look down on you and bark
From the nut trees—
    Wetherbee.   We have them in the Park
Plenty enough. But, say, you aged sinner,
Have you been out much recently at dinner?
    Morrison. What do you mean? You know there's no one here
That dines except ourselves now.
    Wetherbee.   Well, that's queer!
I thought the natives—But I recollect!
It was not reasonable to expect—
    Morrison. What are you driving at?
    Wetherbee.   Oh, nothing much.
But I was thinking how you come in touch
With life at the first dinner in the fall,

When you get back, first, as you can't at all
Later along. But you, of course, won't care
With your idyllic pleasures.
    Morrison.   *Who was there?*
    Wetherbee. Oh—ha, ha! What d'you mean by *there?*
    Morrison.   Come off!
    Wetherbee. What! you remain to pray that came to scoff!
    Morrison. You know what I am after.
    Wetherbee.   Yes, that dinner.
Just a round dozen: Ferguson and Binner
For the fine arts; Bowyer the novelist;
Dr. Le Martin; the psychologist
Fletcher; the English actor Philipson;
The two newspaper Witkins, Bob and John;
A nice Bostonian, Bane the archæologer,
And a queer Russian amateur astrologer;
And Father Gray, the jolly ritualist priest,
And last your humble servant, but not least.
The food was not so filthy, and the wine
Was not so poison. We made out to dine
From eight till one a.m. One could endure
The dinner. But, oh say! *The talk was poor!*
Your natives down at Clamhurst—
    Morrison.   Look ye here!
What date does Thanksgiving come on this year?
    Wetherbee. Why, I suppose—although I don't remember
Certainly—the usual 28th November.

Morrison. Novem—You should have waited to get sober!
It comes on the 11th of October!
And that's to-morrow; and if you happen down
Later, you'd better look for us in town.

THE MOTHER

In the upper chamber of a village house, a young mother lying in bed with her baby on her arm. A nurse moving silently about the room, opens the door softly, and goes out. The mother looks up at the father, who stands looking down on her.

The Mother: Is the nurse gone now? And are we alone
At last?
The Father: Yes, dearest, she is gone; and I
Must leave you, too. You must be quiet, now.
[He goes to the door.
You know, you said if they would let you have
The baby you would go to sleep again
Together. [*Playfully.*] So, now, you must keep your promise!
The Mother: Yes, now I will be quiet. [*After a moment:*]
Dear!
The Father (turning at the door): Yes, dear?
The Mother: See her, how cunningly she nestles down,
As naturally as if she had been used
To doing it for years. How wise she looks!
>   [*The mother rubs her cheek softly against the baby's head, and
>   then draws back her face to look at it. The father comes and
>   stands beside the bed, bending over her and the child.*
How much do you suppose she really knows?
The Father: If she has "newly come from heaven, our
home,"
As Wordsworth says, then she knows everything
We have forgotten, but shall know again.
When we go back to heaven with her.

The Mother: Yes.

> *[She rubs her cheek on the baby's head again.*

Do you believe it?

    The Father: Why, of course I do.
Why, what a—

    The Mother: Nothing. Only, I was wishing
That we might all go on forever here.

    The Father (laughing and then anxiously): Well, I
should not object. But now, my dear,
If you keep up this talking, I am afraid,
You will excite yourself. The doctor said—

    The Mother: Why, I was never calmer in my life!
I feel as if there never could be pain,
Or trouble, or weakness, in the world again.
I am as strong! But, yes, I understand,
And, to please you, I will be quiet now.

> *[She sighs restfully. The father stoops and kisses her and*
> *then the child.*

I wish that you could somehow make one kiss
Do for us both!

    The Father: Well, I should like to try,
Sometime, but now—

    The Mother: Yes, now I must be quiet.
Go! [*He goes toward the door.*] Dear!

> *[He turns again.*

    The Father: Yes, dearest!

    The Mother: But I shall not sleep!
I have been sleeping the whole afternoon.

    The Father (anxiously): Yes, yes, but now you ought to

93

sleep again.
You know the doctor told us—
   The Mother (impatiently): Oh, the doctor!
Does he expect I'll let him take from me
Any more of this time and give it up
To stupid sleep? Why, I want every instant,
To share it all with you, and keep it ours!
   The Father: Yes, love, I know! But now, to keep it ours,
You must do nothing that will make you sick—
   The Mother: And die? Oh, yes! But what if I should die?
I have my baby! What if I should die?
   The Father (wringing his hands):
Dearest, how can you say such things to me?
   The Mother: Well, well! I shall not die. There, go away,
And I will try to sleep. Or no, sit down,
Here by the bed. I will not speak a word.
But it will be more quieting with you
Beside us, than if you were there outside,
Where neither one of us could see you. She
Wants you as much as I.
   The Father (doubtfully drawing up a chair, and then sinking into it): What an idea!
   The Mother: Can't you believe, that through each one of us
She feels and wishes for the other one?
Of course she does!
   The Father: Perhaps.
   The Mother: There's no perhaps.
She'll live her life outside of ours too soon;

And that is why I cannot bear to lose
An instant while she lives it still in ours.
I hate the thought of sleeping.

> *[She suddenly puts out the hand of the arm underlying*
> *the baby's head and clutches the father's hand.*

Where did she
Come from? I do not mean her body or its breath.
That came from us. But oh, her soul, her soul!
Where did that come from?

> *[The father is silent, and she pulls convulsively at his hand.*

Can't you answer me?
The Father (in distress): You know as well as I. Somewhere
in space.
Somewhere in God, she was that which might be,
Among the unspeakable infinitude
Of those that dwell there in the mystery.
The Mother (without releasing her hold): Well!
The Father (with a groan): Well, then our love had some-
how power upon her,
And blindly chose her, that she might become
A living soul, and know, feel, think like us.
It chose her, what she shall be to the end.
The Mother (still clutching his hand):
Out of that infinite beatitude,
Where there is nothing of the consciousness
That we call this and that, here, in the world!
That ignorantly suffers and that dies,
After the life-long fear of death, and goes

Helplessly into that unconsciousness
Again!
 The Father: She is under the same law as we.
But what the law is, or why it should be,
She knows no less or more than we ourselves.
Why do you make me say such things to you?
 The Mother (musingly, and then flinging his hand away):
I heard a woman say once,—years ago,
When I was a young girl, and long before
We saw each other—that it seemed to her
More like our hate than like our love that brought
The children out of that unconsciousness,
Where if there is no life there is no death.
And if there is no joy there is no pain;
But if it was our love that made them come,
Then nothing but its blindness could excuse it.
 The Father: What horrible blasphemy!
 The Mother: How can I tell?
There where our baby was, she was so safe!
And if there seemed no care for her in space,
Or any love, as here sometimes there seems
No care or love for us, where we are left
So to ourselves, our baby never knew it!
 The Father (in anguish): And are you sorry she has come
 to us?
You would rather it had been some other life
Summoned to fill up other lives than ours?
You do not care, then, for our little one?
 The Mother (solemnly): So much that you cannot imagine it.

I was her life, and now she is my life,
My very life, so that if hers went out
Mine would go out with it in the same breath.
That's how I care.

The Father (beseechingly): Oh, try for her sake, then,
If not for yours or mine, to keep from thinking
These dreadful things!

The Mother: Perhaps I do not think them.
Perhaps the baby thinks them.

The Father: No, I am sure,
She does not!

The Mother: But I thought you liked to have me
Think anything that came into my mind,
No matter what about. You used to seem
Proud of my doing it.

The Father: And so I was,
And so I shall be when you are strong enough
To bear it, and when—

The Mother: And when this miracle
No longer is a miracle? No, now,
I must try now to make the meaning out,
While it is still a miracle to me.
You, if you wish, can drug your thoughts, and sleep;
But my thoughts are so precious that if I
Should lose the least of them—What time is it?

[She follows him keenly, as he takes out his watch.
The Father (with a sigh): Daylight, almost. Hark! You can
hear the cocks.

The Mother (smiling): How sweet it is to hear them

crowing so!
It is our own dear earth that seems to speak
In the familiar sound. If it were summer,
The birds would be beginning to sing, now.
I'm glad it is not summer. Is it snowing,
As hard as ever? Look!

The Father (going to the window and peering out): No, it is clear,
And the full moon is shining.

The Mother (lifting her head a little): Let me see!

[With a long sigh, as he draws the curtain:
Yes, it is the moon. The same old moon
We used to walk beneath when we were lovers.
Do you suppose that it was really we?

The Father: If this is we.

[She lets her head drop.

The Mother: It seems a year, almost,
Since yesterday—for now this is tomorrow.
Does the time seem as long to you, I wonder?

The Father (coming back to her): As long as my whole life.

The Mother (taking his hand again): If she could live
Forever on the earth, and we live with her,
I should not fear our having brought her here.
The life of earth, it seems so beautiful,
Far more than anything imaginable
Of any life elsewhere. They cannot hear
Anything like the crowing of the cocks
In heaven—so drowsy and so drowsing! Hark,

How thin and low and faint it is! Oh, sweet,
They keep on calling in their dim, warm barns,
With the kind cattle underneath their roosts,
Munching the hay, and sighing rich and soft.
I used to hear it when I was a child,
And now those things they seem to call me back,
And claim my life a part of theirs again.
I hope that she will live to love such things,
Dear simple things of our dear simple earth.
Do not you, dearest?

  The Father: Yes, indeed I do,
And now if only you could go to sleep —

  The Mother: Well, I will try. I will be quiet now.
How quietly she sleeps! She wants to set
A good example for her worthless mother.
Mother! Just think of it!

  The Father: And father! Think
Of that!

  The Mother: Yes, I have thought of that too, dear.
Put your lips down and kiss her little head.

        [As the father bends over her:
There, now, with your face between hers and mine,
You can be kissing us both.

          [As he lifts himself:
I was just thinking,
What if, instead of our blind, ignorant love,
Choosing her out of the infinitude
Of those unconsciousnesses, as we call them,

She in the wisdom she had right from God,
Had chosen us—in spite of knowing us
Better than we can ever know ourselves,
In all our wickedness and foolishness—
To be her father and her mother here,
Because she understood the good that she
Could do us, and be safe from harm of us:
Would you like that?

The Father: Far better than to think
She came because we ignorantly willed.

The Mother: Well, now, perhaps, that is the way it was,
Only—

The Father: What, dearest?

The Mother: Oh, I do not know
If I can make you understand. Men cannot.
It was not only wishing first to see her,
And willing not to die till I had seen her,
That helped me live through all that agony.
But in the very midst and worst of it
There was a kind of—I can never express it—
Waiting and expectation of a message!
What will her message be?

The Father: Something, perhaps,
That never can be put in words, on earth,
But that we still shall feel the meaning of,
And at the last shall come to understand
As we have always felt it.

The Mother (absently): That will be

The way, no doubt. [*After a moment:*] But there was
    something—as if—
I wish that I could tell you, through it all—
It were I passing into another world,
Where I had never been before. And this,
This is the other world!
    The Father: I do not understand.
    The Mother (sadly): I was afraid of that. And I shall hurt you
If I explain.
    The Father: No, no! You will not hurt me,
Or, if you do, it will be for my good.
    The Mother (after a moment): One day, one little day ago,
If it has been even a day ago,
You were the whole of love, and now you are
The least and last of it, and lost in it.
It is as if you went out of that world,
With that old self of mine, when this new self
Came with our baby here. There, now. I knew it!
I knew that I should hurt you, darling!
    The Father: No.
I am not hurt, and I can understand.
I would not have it different. I should hate
Myself if I could make you care for me
In that old way. It did seem beautiful,
But this—this!
        [*He bends over the mother and child, and gathers them
                                both into his arms.*
    The Mother (putting her hand on his head, and gently

smoothing it):
   There, you'll wake the baby, dearest.
How strange it seems, my saying that already!
But now I am so sleepy, and the doctor
Said that I ought to sleep. You must not mind
If baby and I drive you out of the room?
I must be quiet now. You are not wounded?
                    [She stretches her hand toward him as he rises and
                                        turns toward the door.
   The Father: You could not wound me now, and I believe
We never can wound each other any more,
For she will come between us and will keep us
Safe from each other.
   The Mother: Oh, how sweet you are!
Everything now is clear and right, and you,
You with your love have make it so for me.
Dearest, I am so glad of you and her!
I am so happy and I am so sleepy!
   The Father (catching her hand to his mouth): Go to sleep,
   then, my sleepy, happy love!
Sleep is the best thing even for happiness.
I am going to sleep.
   The Mother (drowsily): Then I will go to sleep.
Father, good-night!
   The Father (joyously): No, no; good-morning, mother.

BLACK CROSS FARM

(To F. S.)

After full many a mutual delay
My friend and I at last fixed on a day
For seeing Black Cross Farm, which he had long
Boasted the fittest theme for tale or song
In all that charming region round about:
Something that must not really be left out
Of the account of things to do for me.
It was a teasing bit of mystery,
He said, which he and his had tried in vain,
Ever since they had found it, to explain.
The right way was to happen, as they did,
Upon it in the hills where it was hid;
But chance could not be always trusted, quite,
You might not happen on it, though you might;
Encores were usually objected to
By chance. The next best thing that we could do
Was in his carry-all, to start together,
And trust that somehow favoring wind and weather,
With the eccentric progress of his horse,
Would so far drift us from our settled course
That we at least could lose ourselves, if not
Find the mysterious object that we sought.
So one blithe morning of the ripe July
We fared, by easy stages, toward the sky
That rested one rim of its turquoise cup

Low on the distant sea, and, tilted up,
The other on the irregular hill-tops. Sweet
The sun and wind that joined to cool and heat
The air to one delicious temperature;
And over the smooth-cropt mowing-pieces pure
The pine breath, borrowing their spicy scent
In barter for the balsam that it lent!
And when my friend handed the reins to me,
And drew a fuming match along his knee,
And lighting his cigar, began to talk,
I let the old horse lapse into a walk
From his perfunctory trot, content to listen,
Amid that leafy rustle and that glisten
Of field, and wood, and ocean, rapt afar,
From every trouble of our anxious star.
From time to time, between effect and cause
In this or that, making a questioning pause,
My friend peered round him while he feigned a gay
Hope that we might have taken the wrong way
At the last turn, and then let me push on,
Or the old horse rather, slanting hither and yon,
And never in the middle of the track,
Except when slanting off or slanting back.
He talked, I listened, while we wandered by
The scanty fields of wheat and oats and rye,
With patches of potatoes and of corn,
And now and then a garden spot forlorn,
Run wild where once a house had stood, or where
An empty house yet stood, and seemed to stare

Upon us blindly from the twisted glass
Of windows that once let no wayfarer pass
Unseen of children dancing at the pane,
And vanishing to reappear again,
Pulling their mother with them to the sight.
Still we kept on, with turnings left and right,
Past farmsteads grouped in cheerful neighborhoods,
Or solitary; then through shadowy woods
Of pine or birch, until the road, grass-grown,
Had given back to Nature all her own
Save a faint wheel-trace, that along the slope,
Rain-gullied, seemed to stop and doubt and grope,
And then quite ceased, as if 't had turned and fled
Out of the forest into which it led,
And left us at the gate whose every bar
Was nailed against us. But, "Oh, here we are!"
My friend cried joyously. "At last, at last!"
And making our horse superfluously fast,
He led the way onward by what had been
A lane, now hid by weeds and briers between
Meadows scarce worth the mowing, to a space
Shaped as by Nature for the dwelling-place
Of kindly human life: a small plateau
Open to the heaven that seemed bending low
In liking for it. There beneath a roof
Still against winter and summer weather-proof,
With walls and doors and windows perfect yet,
Between its garden and its graveyard set,
Stood the old homestead, out of which had perished

105

The home whose memory it dumbly cherished,
And which, when at our push the door swung wide,
We might have well imagined to have died
And had its funeral the day before:
So clean and cold it was from floor to floor,
So lifelike and so deathlike, with the thrill
Of hours when life and death encountered still
Passionate in it. They that lay below
The tangled grasses or the drifted snow,
Husband and wife, mother and little one,
From that sad house less utterly were gone
Than they that living had abandoned it.
In moonless nights their Absences might flit,
Homesick, from room to room, or dimly sit
Around its fireless hearths, or haunt the rose
And lily in the neglected garden close;
But they whose feet had borne them from the door
Would pass the footworn threshold nevermore.
We read the moss-grown names upon the tombs,
With lighter melancholy than the glooms
Of the dead house shadowed us with, and thence
Turning, my heart was pierced with more intense
Suggestion of a mystical dismay,
As in the brilliance of the summer day
We faced the vast gray barn. The house was old,
Though so well kept, as age by years is told
In our young land; but the barn, gray and vast,
Stood new and straight and strong—all battened fast

At every opening; and where once the mow
Had yawned wide-windowed, on the sheathing now
A Cross was nailed, the bigness of a man,
Aslant from left to right, athwart the span,
And painted black as paint could make it. Hushed,
I stood, while manifold conjecture rushed
To this point and to that point, and then burst
In the impotent questionings rejected first.
What did it mean? Ah, that no one could tell.
Who put it there? That was unknown as well.
Was there no legend? My friend knew of none.
No neighborhood story? He had sought for one
In vain. Did he imagine it accident,
With nothing really implied or meant
By the boards set in that way? It might be,
But I could answer that as well as he.
Then (desperately) what did he guess it was:
Something of purpose, or without a cause
Other than chance? He slowly shook his head,
And with his gaze fixed on the symbol said:
"We have quite ceased from guessing or surmising,
For all our several and joint devising
Has left us finally where I must leave you.
But now I think it is your part to do
Yourself some guessing. I hoped you might bring
A fresh mind to the riddle's unraveling.
Come!"

   And thus challenged I could not deny

The sort of right he had to have me try;
And yielding, I began—instinctively
Proceeding by exclusion: "We agree
It was not put there as a pious charm
To keep the abandoned property from harm?
The owner could have been no Catholic;
And yet it was no sacrilegious trick
To make folks wonder; and it was not chance
Assuredly that set those boards askance
In that shape, or before or after, so
Painted them to that coloring of woe.
Do you suppose, then, that it could have been
Some secret sorrow or some secret sin,
That tried to utter or to expiate
Itself in that way: some unhappy hate
Turned to remorse, or some life-rending grief
That could not find in years or tears relief?
Who lived here last?"

                          "Ah," my friend made reply,
"You know as much concerning that as I.
All I could tell is what those gravestones tell,
And they have told it all to you as well.
The names, the dates, the curious epitaphs
At whose quaint phrase one either sighs or laughs,
Just as one's heart or head happens to be
Hollow or not, are there for each to see.
But I believe they have nothing to reveal:
No wrong to publish, no shame to conceal."

"And yet that Cross!" I turned at his reply,
Fixing the silent symbol with my eye,
Insistently. "And you consent," I said,
"To leave the enigma uninterpreted?"

"Why, no," he faltered, then went on: "Suppose
That some one that had known the average woes
Of human nature, finding that the load
Was overheavy for him on life's road,
Had wished to leave some token in this Cross,
Of what had been his gain and been his loss,
Of what had been his suffering and of what
Had also been the solace of his lot?
Whoever that unknown brother-man might be,
I think he must have been like you and me,
Who bear our Cross, and when we fail at length,
Bow down and pray to it for greater strength."

I mused, and as I mused, I seemed to find
The fancy more and still more to my mind.

"Well, let it go at that! I think, for me,
I like that better than some tragedy
Of clearer physiognomy, which were
In being more definite the vulgarer.
For us, what, after all, would be the gain
Of making the elusive meaning plain?
I really think, if I were you and yours,
I would not lift the veil that now obscures
The appealing fact, lest I should spoil the charm.
Deeding me for my own the Black Cross Farm."

"A good suggestion! I am glad," said he,
"We have always practised your philosophy."
    He smiled, we laughed; we sighed and turned away,
And left the mystery to the summer day
That made as if it understood, and could
Have read the riddle to us if it would;
The wide, wise sky, the clouds that on the grass
Let their vague shadows dreamlike trail and pass;
The conscious woods, the stony meadows growing
Up to birch pastures, where we heard the lowing
Of one disconsolate cow. All the warm afternoon,
Lulled in a reverie by the myriad tune
Of insects, and the chirp of songless birds,
Forgetful of the spring-time's lyric words,
Drowsed round us while we tried to find the lane
That to our coming feet had been so plain,
And lost ourselves among the sweetfern's growth,
And thickets of young pine-trees, nothing loath,
Amidst the wilding loveliness to stray,
And spend, if need were, looking for the way,
Whole hours; but blundered into the right course
Suddenly, and came out upon our horse,
Where we had left him—to our great surprise,
Stamping and switching at the pestering flies,
But not apparently anxious to depart,
When nearly overturning at the start,
We followed down that evanescent trace
Which, followed up, had brought us to the place.

Then, all the wayside scenes reversing, we
Dropped to the glimpses of the distant sea,
Content as if we brought, returning thus,
The secret of the Black Cross back with us.

AFTER THE WEDDING

The best room of a village house, after the bride and groom have gone and the wedding guests have left the father and the mother of the bride alone. They are a pair in later middle life with hair beginning to be gray. The father stands at the window staring out. The mother goes restively about, noting this thing and that.

The Mother: I thought we never should be rid of them!
The laughing, and the screaming, and the chatter,
I thought would drive me wild. Now they are gone,
And I can breathe a little while before
I begin putting things in place again.
But what confusion! I should think a whirlwind
Had swept the whole house through, up stairs and down.
It seemed as if those people had no mercy.
And she, before that wall of roses there,
Standing through all so patient and so gentle,
And smiling so on every one that came
To shake hands with her, or to kiss her—white
As the white dress she wore! Ah, no one knew,
As I knew what it cost her to keep up.
I knew her heart was aching for the home
That she was leaving, so that when it came
To the good-by, I almost felt it break
Against my own. Dearest, you do believe
He will be good to her? You do believe—
What are you looking at out of the window?
   The Father, without turning:
At the old slippers they threw after her.

The rice lies in the road as thick as snow.

The Mother: Those silly old customs, how I hate them all!
But if they help to keep our thoughts away—
You do see something else!

The Father: No, nothing else.
I was just wondering if I might not hear
The whistle of their train.

The Mother: And have you heard it?

The Father: Not yet.

The Mother: Then come and sit down here by me,
And tell me how it was when we were married.

> *He comes slowly from the window and stands before her.*

Do you suppose I looked as pale as she did?
I know I did not! I was sure of you
For life and death. Why do not you sit down?

> *He sinks absently beside her on the sofa. She pulls his arm
> round her waist.*

There, now, I do not feel so much afraid!

The Father: Afraid of what?

The Mother: How can I tell you what?
Afraid for her of all that I was then
So radiantly glad of for myself.
Do you believe we really were so happy?
I was one craze of hope and trust in you.
But was that happiness? Do you believe
He will be good to her as you have been
To me?

The Father: Oh, yes.

The Mother: Why do you answer so,

Sighing like that?

The Father: Because men are not good,
As women are.

The Mother: Yes, I kept thinking that,
Through the whole service, when the promises
He made seemed broken in the very making.
How little we know about him! A few months
Since she first saw him, and we give her to him
As trustfully as if we had known him always.

The Father: And we ourselves, we had not known each other
Longer than they when we were married.

The Mother: Oh,
But that was different!

The Father: No, it was the same
And it was like most of the marriages
That have been and that shall be to the end,
They liked the charm of strangeness in each other.

The Mother: But men and women are quite strange enough,
Merely as men and women, to each other,
When they have lived their whole lives long together.
And we ourselves, we took too many chances.
I did not think you ever would be harsh,
And when you spoke the first harsh word to me—
I believe, if he is ever unkind to her,
That I shall know it, wherever it may be.
She will come to me somehow in her grief,
And let me comfort her poor ghost with mine,
For it would kill us both. Do you suppose—
Do you believe he ever will be harsh

With her?

The Father: I almost think you ask me that
Just to torment me.

The Mother: There, that is so like you!
You cannot talk of her as if she were
A woman after all. But, I can tell you,
She in her turn can bear all I have borne;
And though she seems so frail and sensitive,
She is not one to break at a mere touch.
But men are that way, I have noticed it;
They think their wives can endure everything,
Their daughters nothing. You are not listening!

The Father: Yes, I am listening. What is it you mean?

The Mother: You are tenderer of your children than your
    wives
Because you love what is yourselves in them,
And you must love somebody else in us.
Cannot you give me a moment's sympathy
Now when I have nobody left but you?
What are you thinking of, I'd like to know?

*The Father, going back to the window and kneeling on the
        window-seat, with his forehead against the pane:*
The night when she was born.

The Mother: I knew it! I
Was thinking of it too, and how it seemed
As if she had somehow chosen us to be
Her father and her mother.

The Father: Why not him,

Then, for her husband, by a mystery
As sacred?

 The Mother: Oh, why do you ask? Because
There is no other world, now, as there was
Then, where the mystery could shape itself—
No hitherto, as there is no hereafter.
We have destroyed it for ourselves and her,
And love for all of us is as much a thing
Of earth as death itself.

 The Father: I never said
That world did not exist.

 The Mother: Oh, no, you only
Said that you did not know, and I have only
Bettered your ignorance a little and said
I knew. Women must have some faith or other,
Even if they make a faith of disbelief;
They cannot halt half-way in yes and no;
And she is more like me than you in that,
Though she is like you in so many things.
That shattered fantasy—or, what you please—
Cannot be mended now and used again;
And howsoever she has chosen him,—
Or, if you like, he has been chosen for her,—
The choice is made between his love and ours.
The home she seemed to bring, then, when she came,
Now is gone, it lies here in the dust.
Oh, I can pick the house up, after while,
But never pick the home up, while I live!

Well, let it be! I suppose you will call it
Nature, and preach that cold philosophy
Of yours; that every home is founded on
The ruin of some other home and shall be
The ruin out of which still other homes
Shall grow in turn, and so on to the end.
I find no comfort in it, and my heart
Aches for the child that is not less my child
Because she is her husband's wife. Oh, yes,
If we were two fond optimistic fools,
I dare say we should sit here in this horror,
And hold each other's hands and smile to think
Of what a brilliant wedding it had been;
How everybody said how well she looked,
And how he was so handsome and so manly;
And try to follow them in imagination
To their new house, and settle them in it;
And say how soon we would be hearing from her,
And then how soon they would come back to us
Next summer. But we have not been that kind.
We have always said the things we really thought,
And not shrunk from the facts; and now I face them,
And say this wedding—Hark! was that their train?
    The Father: It is the freight mounting the grade. Their
    train
Is overdue, but it will soon be there.
    The Mother: If it would never come or never go!
If all the worlds that whir around the sun

Could stop, and none of them go on again!
Once I had courage for us both, and now
You ought to have it. Oh, say something, do,
To help me bear it!

The Father: What is it I should say!

The Mother: That it has been all my own doing! Say
That I would have it, and am like the mothers,
The stupid mothers, still uncivilized,
That wish their daughters married for the sake
Of being married: that would help me bear it.
If you blamed me then I could blame you too,
And say you wished it quite as much as I.

The Father: We neither of us wished it, and I think
We have always blamed each other needlessly.

The Mother: Yes, and I cannot bear it as I used
When she was with us. Now that she is gone
And you are all in all to me again,
Dearest, you must be very good to me.
Did you hear something?

The Father, going to the window:

                              Yes, I thought I heard
The coming of their train; but it was nothing.

The Mother, unheedingly: The worst of all was having to
    part so—
Hurried and fluttered—up there in her room,
Where she had been so long our little child,
And with that hubbub going on down here,
Not realize that we were parting. Oh,
If we could only have had a little time

And quiet for it! Hark! What noise was that?

    The Father: What noise?

    The Mother: Something that sounded like a voice!

Her voice! I know it must have been her voice!

                   She rushes to the window and stares out.

I always knew within my heart that she

Would call for me, if any unhappiness

Greater than she could bear should come to her.

    The Father: But what unhappiness—

    The Mother: A tone, a look!

    The Father: With our arms round her yet? He could not. That

Would be against nature.

    The Mother: Nature! How you men

Are always thinking about nature! Little

You understand her! Nature flatters men.

She gives men mastery and health and life,

And women subjection, weakness, pain and death.

We know what nature is and you know nothing.

She takes our youth and wastes it upon you,

She steals our beauty for you, and she uses

Our love itself to enslave us to you. Nature!

    The Father: Has it been really so with you and me?

    The Mother: How do I know? You may have been unlike

Other men.

    The Father: No, but quite like other men;

Not better. Shall she take her chance with him?

Speak out now from the worst you know of me,

And say if you would have her back again.

The Mother: It keeps on calling! Can it be her voice?

The Father: Then say it is her voice. What will you answer?
Shall she come home and be our child again?

The Mother: You put it all on me!

The Father: Then if I take
The burden all upon myself, and choose—

The Mother: What?

The Father: That her longing for us should have power
To bring her back?

The Mother: To say good-by again?

The Father: To stay and never say good-by again,
To leave her husband and to cleave to us.

The Mother: I cannot let you choose! For oh! it seems
That it would really happen if you chose.
Wait, wait a minute, while I try to think,
How would it be, if she came back again,
And crept once more into this empty shell
Of life that has been lived! What is there here,
But two old hearts that hardly have enough
Of love left for each other? And she needs
The whole of such love as I found in you
When I had given you all the love I had.
No, she must go with him as I with you.
Because she has been all in all to us
So long, and yet for such a little time,
We have come to think that she must be unlike
Others, and she must be above their fate.
But that is foolish. She must take her chance,

120

As I took mine, and as we women have
Taken our chance from the beginning. There!
I give her up for the first time and last!
Tell her— I talk as if you were with her
There, and not here with me!

The Father: And I—I feel
As if we both were there with her and with
Each other here.

The Mother: And so we shall be always;
And most with her when most we are alone,
See, they have mounted to their train together!
She stands a moment at the door and waves
The hand that is not held in his towards us—
And they are gone into their unknown world
To find our own past in their future there!

We had gone down at Christmas, where our host
Had opened up his house on the Maine coast,
For the week's holidays, and we were all,
On Christmas night, sitting in the great hall,
About the corner fireplace, while we told
Stories like those that people, young and old,
Have told at Christmas firesides from the first,
Till one who crouched upon the hearth, and nursed
His knees in his claspt arms, threw back his head,
And fixed our host with laughing eyes, and said,
"This is so good, here—with your hickory logs
Blazing like natural-gas ones on the dogs,
And sending out their flicker on the wall
And rafters of your mock-baronial hall,
All in fumed-oak, and on your polished floor,
And the steel-studded panels of your door—
I think you owe the general make-believe
Some sort of story that will somehow give
A more ideal completeness to our case,
And make each several listener in his place—
Or hers—sit up, with a real goose-flesh creeping
All over him—or her—in proper keeping
With the locality and hour and mood.
Come!"
            And amid the cries of "Yes!" and "Good!"
Our host laughed back; then, with a serious air,
Looked around him on our hemicycle, where

He sat midway of it. "Why," he began,
But interrupted by the other man,
He paused for him to say:

> "Nothing remote,
But something with the actual Yankee note
Of here and now in it!"

> "I'll do my best,"
Our host replied, "to satisfy a guest.
What do you say to Barberry Cove? And would
Five years be too long since?"

> "No: both are good.
Go on!"

> "You noticed that big house to-day
Close to the water, and the sloop that lay,
Stripped for the winter, there, beside the pier?
Well, there she has lain just so, year after year;
And she will never leave her pier again,
But once, each spring she sailed in sun or rain,
For Bay Chaleur—or Bay Shaloor, as they
Like better to pronounce it down this way."

"I like Shaloor myself rather the best.
But go ahead," said the exacting guest.
And with a glance around at us that said,
"Don't let me bore you!" our host went ahead.

"Captain Gilroy built the big house, and he
Still lives there with his aging family.
He built the sloop, and when he used to come
Back from the Banks he made her more his home
With his two boys, than the big house. The two

Made up with him a good half of her crew,
Until it happened, on the Banks, one day
The oldest boy got in a steamer's way,
And went down in his dory. In the fall
The others came without him. That was all
That showed in either one of them except
That now the father and the brother slept
Ashore, and not on board. When the spring came
They sailed for the old fishing-ground the same
As ever. Yet, not quite the same. The brother,
If you believed what folks say, kissed his mother
Good-by in going; and by general rumor,
The father, so far yielding as to humor
His daughters' weakness, rubbed his stubbly cheek
Against their lips. Neither of them would speak,
But the dumb passion of their love and grief
In so much show at parting found relief.

"The weeks passed and the months. Some times they heard
At home, by letter, from the sloop, or word
Of hearsay from the fleet. But by and by
Along about the middle of July,
A time in which they had no news began,
And holding unbrokenly through August, ran
Into September. Then, one afternoon,
While the world hung between the sun and moon,
And while the mother and her girls were sitting
Together with their sewing and their knitting,—
Before the early-coming evening's gloom

Had gathered round them in the living-room,
Helplessly wondering to each other when
They should hear something from their absent men,—
They saw, all three, against the window-pane,
A face that came and went, and came again,
Three times, as though for each of them, about
As high up from the porch's floor without
As a man's head would be that stooped to stare
Into the room on their own level there.
Its eyes dwelt on them wistfully as if
Longing to speak with the dumb lips some grief
They could not speak. The women did not start
Or scream, though each one of them, in her heart,
Knew she was looking on no living face,
But stared, as dumb as it did, in her place."

Here our host paused, and one sigh broke from all
Our circle whom his tale had held in thrall.
But he who had required it of him spoke
In what we others felt an ill-timed joke:
"Well, this is something like!" A girl said, "Don't!"
As if it hurt, and he said, "Well, I won't.
Go on!" And in a sort of muse our host
Said, "I suppose we all expect a ghost
Will sometimes come to us. But I doubt if we
Are moved by its coming as we thought to be.
At any rate, the women were not scared,
But, as I said, they simply sat and stared
Till the face vanished. Then the mother said,

'It was your father, girls, and he is dead.'
But both had known him; and now all went on
Much as before till three weeks more were gone,
When, one night sitting as they sat before,
Together with their mother, at the door
They heard a fumbling hand, and on the walk
Up from the pier, the tramp and muffled talk
Of different wind-blown voices that they knew
For the hoarse voices of their father's crew.
Then the door opened, and their father stood
Before them, palpably in flesh and blood.
The mother spoke, for all, her own misgiving:
'Father, is this your ghost? Or are you living?'
'I am alive!' 'But in this very place
We saw your face look, like a spirit's face,
There through that window, just three weeks ago,
And now you are alive!' 'I did not know
That I had come; all I know is that then
I wanted to tell you folks here that our Ben
Was dying of typhoid fever. He raved of you
So that I could not think what else to do
He's there in Bay Shaloor!'

     "Well, that's the end."
And rising up to mend the fire our friend
Seemed trying to shun comment; but in vain:
The exacting guest came at him once again;
"You must be going to fall down, I thought,
There at the climax, when your story brought

The skipper home alive and well. But no,
You saved yourself with honor."
                              The girl said, "Oh,"
Who spoke before, "it's wonderful! But you,
How could you think of anything so true,
So delicate, as the father's wistful face
Coming there at the window in the place
Of the dead son's! And then, that quaintest touch,
Of half-apology—that he felt so much,
He *had* to come! How perfectly New England! Well,
I hope nobody will undertake to tell
A common or garden ghost-story to-night."
    Our host had turned again, and at her light
And playful sympathy he said, "My dear,
I hope that no one will imagine here
I have been inventing in the tale that's done.
My little story's charm if it has one
Is from no skill of mine. One does not change
The course of fable from its wonted range
To such effect as I have seemed to do:
Only the fact could make my story true."

It was against the law, in such case made and provided,
Of the United States, but by the good will of the pilots
That we would some of us climb to the pilot-house after our
    breakfast
For a morning smoke, and find ourselves seats on the
    benching
Under the windows, or in the worn-smooth armchairs. The
    pilot,
Which one it was did not matter, would tilt his head round
    and say, "All right!"
When he had seen who we were, and begin, or go on as
    from stopping
In the midst of talk that was leading up to a story,
Just before we came in, and the story, begun or beginning,
Always began or ended with some one, or something or
    other,
Having to do with the river. If one left the wheel to the
    other,
Going off watch, he would say to his partner standing
    behind him
With his hands stretched out for the spokes that were not
    given up yet,
"Captain, you can tell them the thing I was going to tell them
Better than I could, I reckon," and then the other would
    answer,
"Well, I don't know as I feel so sure of that, captain," and
    having

Recognized each other so by that courtesy title of captain
Never officially failed of without offense among pilots,
One would subside into Jim and into Jerry the other.

　　It was on these terms, at least, Captain Dunn relieved
　　　　Captain Davis
When we had settled ourselves one day to listen in comfort,
After some psychological subtleties we had indulged in at
　　breakfast
Touching that weird experience every one knows when the
　　senses
Juggle the points of the compass out of true orientation,
Changing the North to the South, and the East to the West.
　　"Why, Jerry, what was it
You was going to tell them?" "Oh, never *you* mind what it
　　was, Jim.
You tell them something else," and so Captain Davis
　　submitted,
While Captain Dunn, with a laugh, got away beyond reach
　　of his protest.
Then Captain Davis, with fitting, deprecatory preamble,
Launched himself on a story that promised to be all a story
Could be expected to be, when one of those women—
　　you know them—
Who interrupt on any occasion or none, interrupted,
Pointed her hand, and asked, "Oh, what is that island there,
　　captain?"
"That one, ma'am?" He gave her the name, and then the
　　woman persisted,

"Don't say you know them all by sight!" "Yes, by sight or by
    feeling."
"What do you mean by feeling?" "Why, just that by daylight
    we see them,
And in the dark it's like as if somehow we felt them, I reckon.
Every foot of the channel and change in it, wash-out and
    cave-in,
Every bend and turn of it, every sand-bar and landmark,
Every island, of course, we have got to see them, or feel them."
"But if you don't?" "But we've got to." "But aren't you ever
    mistaken?"
"Never the second time." "Now, what do you mean,
    Captain Davis?
Never the second time." "Well, let me tell you a story.
It's not the one I begun, but that island you asked about
    yonder
Puts me in mind of it, happens to be the place where it
    happened,
Three years ago. I suppose no man ever knew the Ohio
Better than Captain Dunlevy, if any one else knew it like
    him.
Man and boy he had been pretty much his whole life on the
    river:
Cabin-boy first on a keelboat before the day of the steam-
    boats,
Back in the pioneer times; and watchman then on a steam-
    boat;
Then second mate, and then mate, and then pilot and
    captain and owner—

But he was proudest, I reckon, of being about the best
   pilot
On the Ohio. He knew it as well as he knew his own Bible,
And I don't hardly believe that ever Captain Dunlevy
Let a single day go by without reading a chapter."

   While the pilot went on with his talk, and in regular,
      rhythmical motion
Swayed from one side to the other before his wheel, and we
   listened,
Certain typical facts of the picturesque life of the river
Won their way to our consciousness as without help of our
   senses.
It was along about the beginning of March, but already
In the sleepy sunshine the budding maples and
   willows,
Where they waded out in the shallow wash of the freshet,
Showed the dull red and the yellow green of their blossoms
   and catkins,
And in their tops the foremost flocks of blackbirds debated
As to which they should colonize first. The indolent
   house-boats
Loafing along the shore, sent up in silvery spirals
Out of their kitchen pipes the smoke of their casual
   breakfasts.
Once a wide tow of coal-barges, loaded clear down to the
   gunwales,
Gave us the slack of the current, with proper formalities
   shouted

By the hoarse-throated stern-wheeler that pushed the black
  barges before her,
And as she passed us poured a foamy cascade from her paddles.
Then, as a raft of logs, which the spread of the barges had
  hidden,
River-wide, weltered in sight, with a sudden jump forward
  the pilot
Dropped his whole weight on the spokes of the wheel just
  in time to escape it.

  "Always give those fellows," he joked, "all the leeway
      they ask for;
Worst kind of thing on the river you want your boat to run
  into.
Where had I got about Captain Dunlevy? Oh yes, I remember.
Well, when the railroads began to run away from the steam-
  boats,
Taking the carrying trade in the very edge of the water,
It was all up with the old flush times, and Captain Dunlevy
Had to climb down with the rest of us pilots till he was only
Captain the same as any and every pilot is captain,
Glad enough, too, to be getting his hundred and twenty-
  five dollars
Through the months of the spring and fall while navigation
  was open.
Never lowered himself, though, a bit from captain and
  owner,
Knew his rights and yours, and never would thought of
  allowing

Any such thing as a liberty *from* you or taking one *with* you.
I had been his cub, and all that I knew of the river
Captain Dunlevy had learnt me; and if you know what the
    feeling
Is of a cub for the pilot that learns him the river, you'll trust
    me
When I tell you I felt it the highest kind of an honor
Having him for my partner; and when I came up to relieve
    hirn,
One day, here at the wheel, and actu'lly thought that I
    found him
Taking that island there on the left, I thought I was crazy.
No, I couldn't believe my senses, and yet I couldn't endure it.
Seeing him climb the spokes of the wheel to warp the
    Kanawha,
With the biggest trip of passengers ever she carried,
Round on the bar at the left that fairly stuck out of the
    water.
Well, as I said, he learnt me all that I knew of the river,
And was I to learn *him* now which side to take of an island
When I knew he knew it like his right hand from his left
    hand?
My, but I hated to speak! It certainly seemed like my tongue
    clove,
Like the Bible says, to the roof of my mouth! But I had to.
'Captain,' I says, and it seemed like another person was talking,
'Do you usu'lly take that island there on the eastward?'
'Yes,' he says, and he laughed, 'and I thought I had learnt
    you to do it,

133

When you was going up.' 'But not going *down*, did you,
    captain?'
'Down?' And he whirled at me, and, without ever stopping
    his laughing,
Turned as white as a sheet, and his eyes fairly bulged from
    their sockets.
Then he whirled back again, and looked up and down on
    the river,
Like he was hunting out the shape of the shore and the
    landmarks.
Well, I suppose the thing has happened to every one some-
    time,
When you find the points of the compass have swapped
    with each other,
And at the instant you're looking, the North and the South
    have changed places.
I knew what was in his mind as well as Dunlevy himself did.
Neither one of us spoke a word for nearly a minute.
Then in a kind of whisper he says, 'Take the wheel, Captain
    Davis!'
Let the spokes fly, and while I made a jump forwards to
    catch them,
Staggered into that chair—well, the very one you are in,
    ma'am.
Set there breathing quick, and, when he could speak, all he
    said was,
'This is the end of it for me on the river, Jim Davis,'
Reached up over his head for his coat where it hung by that
    window,

Trembled onto his feet, and stopped in the door there a
    second,
Stared in hard like as if for good-by to the things he was
    used to,
Shut the door behind him, and never come back again
    through it."
While we were silent, not liking to prompt the pilot with
    questions,
"Well," he said, at last, "it was no use to argue. We tried it,
In the half-hearted way that people do that don't mean it.
Every one was his friend here on the *Kanawha,* and *we* knew
It was the first time he ever had lost his bearings, but *he*
    knew,
In such a thing as that, that the first and the last are the same
    time.
When we had got through trying our worst to persuade
    him, he only
Shook his head and says, 'I am done for, boys, and you
    know it,'
Left the boat at Wheeling, and left his life on the river—
Left his life on the earth, you may say, for I don't call it
    living,
Setting there homesick at home for the wheel he can never
    go back to.
Reads the river-news regular; knows just the stage of the
    water
Up and down the whole way from Cincinnati to Pittsburg;
Follows every boat from the time she starts out in the
    spring-time

Till she lays up in the summer, and then again in the winter;
Wants to talk all about her and who is her captain and pilot;
Then wants to slide away to that everlastingly puzzling
Thing that happened to him that morning on the *Kanawha*
When he lost his bearings and North and South had
    changed places—
No, I don't call that living, whatever the rest of you call it."
We were silent again till that woman spoke up, "And what
    was it,
Captain, that kept him from going back and being a pilot?"
"Well, ma'am," after a moment the pilot patiently answered,
"*I* don't hardly believe that I could explain exactly."

CONTEMPORARIES

[TO JOHN BURROUGHS]

From blossomed boughs and nesting birds,
   From springing grass and new-turned furrows,
With love too great for forward words,
   All nature hails her son, John Burroughs.

A DOUBLE-BARRELLED SONNET TO MARK TWAIN

(Written to be heard, not read)

I

First Barrel

The man whose birthday we renown tonight
    Unites all heads and hearts in one acclaim
    As never any other "heir of fame":
The missionary may not love him quite,
The imperialist may not think him wholly right.
    The predatory cabman free from blame,
    The moralist consider it the same
To teach by joke as with a text in sight.
Some as a scientist may not prize him much;
    Some may deny him the true lyric leaven
As poet; some the fine old Bewick touch
    As wood engraver; but none under heaven,
Of all his critics, or those who pose as such,
    Gainsay him the glory of being sixty-seven.

II

Second Barrel

"Oh, no! Hold on!" I hear his voice implore,
    "You are mistaken; it is not the case
    The Colonel, to save the Sabbath from disgrace,
Calls this my birthday. But, in fact, before
The thirtieth—and there still are two days more—
You cannot make me more than sixty-six."
    "In vain!" the inexorable Muse replies.

"It may be so; but as the executrix
    Of your own theory of convenient lies,
I must insist upon the Colonel's date.
Besides, what matter whether soon or late
    Your birthday comes whose fame all dates defies?
Still, to have everything beyond cavil right,
We will dine with you here till Sunday night."

THE AMERICAN JOKE

*(Read at the Birthday Dinner to S. L. Clemens,
December 5, 1905)*

I

A traveller from the Old World, just escaped
    Our Customs with his life, had found his way
To a place up-town, where a Colossus shaped
    Itself, sky-scraper high, against the day.
A vast smile, dawning from his mighty lips,
    Like sunshine on its visage seemed to brood;
One eye winked in perpetual eclipse,
    In the other a huge tear of pity stood.
Wisdom in nuggets round its temples shone;
    Its measureless bulk grotesque, exultant, rose;
And while Titanic puissance clothed it on,
    Patience with foreigners was in its pose.
So that, "What are thou?" the emboldened traveller spoke,
And it replied, "I am the American Joke.

II

"I am the joke that laughs the proud to scorn;
    I mock at cruelty, I banish care,
I cheer the lowly, chipper the forlorn,
    I bid the oppressor and hypocrite beware,
I tell the tale that makes men cry for joy;
    I bring the laugh that has no hate in it;
In the heart of age I wake the undying boy;
    My big stick blossoms with a thornless wit,

The lame dance with delight in me; my mirth
  Reaches the deaf untrumpeted; the blind
My point can see. I jolly the whole earth,
  But most I love to jolly my own kind,
Joke of a people great, gay, bold, and free,
I type their master-mood. *Mark Twain made me.*"

TO A GREAT EDITOR

In every human life, however filled
    With obvious proofs of wisdom and of good,
The vaster part is void to minds unskilled
    In sense of things less seen than understood;
And they who know you only by the things
    That you have done, or suffered to be done,
Know you not, Alden, in the inmost springs
    Of soul that rather shun than seek the sun;
Poet, more poet for beauty than for fame,
    Sage for the sake of being, not seeming wise,
Preacher of truth, and not of praise or blame,
    Critic whose law inspires as well as tries,
You who have deepened and enlarged your day,
    You shall remain when it has passed away.

* Henry Mills Alden

[THOMAS BAILEY ALDRICH]

Not here, where that quick, subtle spirit of his
    With many a smile and many a nodded jest
    Seemed to escape us when we praised our best,
Could he be wholly what he was and is.
But in the simple house where once he dwelt,
    Amidst the old fashioned Portsmouth neighborhood
    In days when all of life was glad and good,
He will be willing to be known and felt;
A soul attuned to music, and a mind
    Mystically vowed to beauty, in an art
    That tirelessly upon itself refined:
Less of the school than of the poet heart,
There in his earliest and his latest home
He hospitably waits and bids us come.

What has become of it, your youth and mine,
That once we drank together like a wine,
And while we kissed the brimming bowl and quaffed,
Joked at ourselves, and laughed, and laughed, and laughed.

Even the antic echo of our mirth,
Gay shadow of it, has perished from the earth,
And silence has fallen where there used to be
The joyousness of the prime for you and me.

You have taken it with you whither you have gone,
And I, who here behind you, linger on,
Make it my cheer that in whatever far
Planet you dwell, our youth and gladness are.

[JOSEPH A. HOWELLS]

Stone, upon which with hands of boy and man
   He framed the history of his time until,
Week after week the varying record ran
   To its half-centuried tale of well and ill.

Remember now how true through all those days
   He was: friend, brother, husband, father, son;
Fill the whole limit of your space with praise;
   There needs no room for blame: blame there was none.

POEMS, 1902–1916

THE CHRISTMAS SPIRIT

I

About the end of August, one hot day,
As on the new-mown rowan grass I lay
Under the ash whose flickering foliage made
A crazy-quilt of sunshine and of shade
For that soft bed, there came up from the sea
A curious figure floundering on toward me.
His coat looked somewhat like a coat of mail,
And somewhat like a weather-beaten sail;
His fluffy hair and beard were white as foam
That crests the curling breakers when they comb
Upon the beach, with glints of that cold green
Which through the water's shattering bulk is seen,
Showing itself within; and all without
His head was rudely garlanded about
With what at first seemed sea-weed. In his hand
He bore, to help his steps, a sturdy wand,
And as he wavered up my ragged lawn,
He looked like Neptune with his sea-legs on,
Using his trident for a walking-stick;
And then my vision played itself the trick
Of finding hitched below my sagging pier
The god's sea-chariot with its team of queer
Sea-horses resting in the gentle surf,
And browsing on the edges of the turf
There tangled with the tresses of the moss
That round the wave-worn ledges sway and toss.

All this I saw with half-shut, dreamy eyes,
To which it did not bring the least surprise,
And without troubling to get up and greet
My unexpected visitor on my feet,
"Chaire, Poseidon!" I began to speak,
Lazily hailing him in his native Greek
(*Chaire,* I will interpret, means *Hello,*
Or at least Arnold's First Book taught me so),
And then as he came staggering through my clover,
"Sit down, old fellow; you seem half-seas-over,
Even on the shore," I added for a joke,
Always acceptable to seafaring folk.
But suddenly, to my astonishment,
Up-straightening from the staff on which he leant,
He thundered, after an indignant pause,
"Poseidon nothing! I am Santa Claus!"

II

    The thunder of his tones was somewhat cracked,
But otherwise I cannot say he lacked
A certain majesty, and I own he made
Me involuntarily sit up. Dismayed,
But bound he should not think he had frightened me,
I forced a laugh, and answered mockingly:
"What are you giving me? At this time of year,
You, Santa Claus! What are you doing here,
Full four months before Christmas? Ah, come off!"
He faltered, as if daunted by the scoff,

And I pursued: "Neptune, this will not do;
If you are Santa Claus, and are not you,
Where are his emblems?" "Where are his emblems, man?"
With renewed self-possession he began,
"If these are not his emblems, what are these?
This stifling beard and wig, and, if you please,
This wreath of ground-pine? This fur overcoat—
White rabbit edging on a ground of goat?—
And these abominable rubber boots
That stumble with me on your rowan roots,
Worse than they ever do through drifted snow?
And this long whip-stock? And down there below
Under your pier, whose faithful reindeer wait,
With whose accustomed sledge and well-known freight
Of Christmas goods?—the same old sweets and toys,
For those same everlasting girls and boys!
Which is their best way up?" I looked again,
And saw that he was right. It was as plain
As could be to that second glance, and I
Humbled myself to make a fit reply.
I owned the break that I had made, but pleaded,
With somewhat more prolixity than needed,
How the remarkable resemblance had
Deluded me. Yet it was not so bad:
Neptune was of an ancient family,
And there were several much worse gods than he.
"A *heathen* god!" Santa Claus frowned and puffed;
But I perceived that he was not so huffed

As if 't had been some low-down demi-god.
"Of course," I said, "but it was not so odd,
Here by the sea-shore," and I tried to make
The saint confess the logic of my break;
And when I thought I had him pacified,
I said 'twould always be a source of pride
With me that he had called upon me here
At this—for him—unpleasant time of year.
What did I owe the honor— With a bellow,
"Have you forgot?" the violent old fellow
Demanded, and although I well could pardon
Much to the heat, and would not have been hard on
Any one who had lost his temper on a day
Like that if dressed in his peculiar way,
Still, it makes one always feel rather rotten
To be reminded that he has forgotten.
I roared, "Forgotten what?" in fierce disdain,
And then was daunted when he came again.
"Forgotten? Well, I am glad to have you hear it:
You were to write about The Christmas Spirit
For the next Christmas number of the WEEKLY.
And I would counsel you to take it meekly.
I come as editorially appointed,
And I do not propose to be aroynted."
"All in good time," I answered, hardily.
"As to the promised paper, I agree.
But why should I write of the Christmas Spirit
In the hot heart of midsummer, or near it?"

"Because," he said, "if you will keep your patience!
They have arranged for copious illustrations,
And these take time, as you yourself must own,
Even with reproductions in half-tone,
And still more time if they decide to print
The illustrations in some sort of tint.
Bring out your kodak-fiend, then, and I'll get
My team of reindeer up out of the wet."
He seemed to think that he had made a joke,
And his old bleared eyes twinkled as he spoke,
And turned to go for them. And I arose,
And leaning on the tree, assumed a pose.
But "Wait!" I said. "One moment, my dear friend!
You may be Santa Claus, as you pretend.
You look it, somewhat, but as Santa Claus
You are no nearer than Poseidon was
To the true Christmas Spirit. Oh, I know
What you will say about the new-fallen snow,
And stockings by the chimney, and the trees
Hung with the tinselled overflow from these,
Mistletoe, ground-pine, holly wreaths, and all
The garnish for the transoms and the hall;
Presents of every sort, and Christmas geese
And turkeys for the poor, to leave in peace
The rich man with his conscience; for the bowl
Of wassail general liquors, and the whole
Catalogue of your holiday paraphernalia
Borrowed for Christmas from the Saturnalia

You used to riot in, you ancient fraud,
Who turn your nose up at a heathen god—
Look at your nose!" The feat was difficult,
And he attempted it without result;
But *I* looked at it, and I made it turn
From purple-red to crimson-red and burn
To a dull ashen-gray in the fierce blaze
Shot from my highly concentrated gaze.
"Look at your cheeks!" I shouted, "with that net
Of pimples and congested veins that fret
Their surfaces; and if you would despise
Yourself as you deserve, look at your eyes,
Bloodshot with drunkenness and gluttony!
Then drop your glance, in utter shame, and see
The tremulous, pendulous paunch that has displaced
Anything like the semblance of a waist
You ever had! You old, profane buffoon,
With a face like a dissipated moon,
You dare to call yourself the Christmas Spirit?
Off of my grass! Get your reindeer and clear it
Off of my beach, before I go and bring
Action against you all for trespassing!
You call yourself the Christmas Spirit, you
Who never imagined anything to do
At Christmas-tide, except on Christmas eve,
Mock with bright dreams the children who believe
That you come down the chimney, and then fright
Their surfeit with nightmares all Christmas night;

And at those awful early family dinners
Inspire the saints to gormandize like sinners,
And in the riot to which you have won them
Lose all the good the sermon might have done them;
Who fill the Christmas week with every folly,
And bring the New Year in with melancholy
Thoughts of bills payable, and the ruinous rifts
Made in men's pocket-books by Christmas gifts
Not blessed to her who thought she had to give
More than they were to him who must receive!
And do you fancy that you are the type
Of that which was fulfilled when time was ripe,
And peace was promised upon all the earth,
And unto men good-will with that great Birth
Which angels, thronging from the upper skies,
Prophesied in their glad antiphonies?
Off, hoary trifler! What have such as you
With sacred memories like these to do!
Poor, pagan outcast, derelict forlorn!
Back, with the perished gods and creeds outworn
From which you came, back into eldest night!
Or, if you still must haunt this age of light,
Look well about you, see what has been done:
How life smiles everywhere beneath the sun;
See the whole world at peace, from the Transvaal
To the far Philippines, one rapture all
Of peace with freedom. Ev'n the Europeans,
By the decision of their kings and queens,

Are getting ready to lay down their arms.
The sea no longer quakes at the alarms
Of the embattled fleets: each fell machine
Embodied in the mercantile marine,
The Trusts' rich products bears from shore to shore,
And blesses lands it bullies now no more.
No more the poor toil for starvation's wage;
No more the incorporate employers rage
At strikes, and outside hints of arbitration:
Prosperity is shared by the whole nation.
No famishing woman now need sell herself,
No man part with his principles for pelf
To bribe the wolf that used to haunt the door.
Especially, in the Southern States, no more
The little child watches the whirring loom
Weaving into the web its life's young bloom;
No more at Newport by the sad sea wave,
Divorce digs in the sand love's soon lost grave.
"Can you look round on such a state as this,
And fail to see how much you come amiss?
How utterly superfluous you are
In the economy of this happy star?
Away with you! Or, if you still would choose
To stay, and try to make yourself of use,
Amidst a world of busy people, each
Striving to practice what the others preach,
Lay off these foolish symbols with your coat
(I'm glad you were frank enough to own it goat),

158

Leave guttling, guzzling, set a good example—
You'll find the opportunity is ample,
For with the spread of our prosperity,
We are all in risk of victualling too free—
Put from you far the homes of wealth and pride,
And spend your days doing good on the East Side.
From your old ways return, reform, repent,
And be what the true Christmas Spirit meant!"

III

    At these stern words I looked to see him shrink
Struck through and through with bitter shame, and sink
Before me. And at first he did seem taken
Rather aback, and turned, a good deal shaken,
As if in silence to depart; and then
He turned and meekly fronted me again;
And as he spoke he seemed to gather force
And held with rising dignity his course.
"The Christmas Spirit did I say I was?
I only said that I was Santa Claus!
And very likely, if your supposition
Holds, I am but a childish superstition;
Yes, very probably, I used to be
No better than a pagan deity,—
Not one of the swell gods, but of the sort
That went about the country to resort
Among the lanes in rustic neighborhoods,
The meadows, and the depths of twilight woods,
Befriending the poor husbandman and shepherd

Whose fields and folds and homes the wild things jeopard.
But I have been converted and baptized,
And I should be considerably surprised
If some born Christians had a better claim
Than I can urge—not boast—to wear the name.
I will not speak of any good I do—
I leave all that to moralists like you;
But, in the course of pleasure, once a year,
I come to bring men's hearths a little cheer;
To scatter here and there a little kindness;
A little deafness and a little blindness
To one another's faults among you mortals;
And not distinguishing between your portals—
Or chimneys, rather—in my rounds I try
To visit rich and poor alike; for I,
Strange as it may appear, have found, indeed,
Every one living lives somehow in need
Of help, of comfort, and even of that jollity
You seem to have no use for in your polity.
Since you are virtuous, shall there be no more
Of cakes and ale? Aye, but there shall, galore!
I will see to it, with both meat and drink—
Oh, by-the-way! Now that I come to think,
What *are* your virtues?" Here the saint broke off
With what appeared a very sinful scoff
Lurking in bearded mouth and winking eye.
Ere I could frame a suitable reply
He turned, unceremonious, on his heel,
And stumbled through the rowan with a peal

Of mocking laughter, downward to my beach,
Which with few giant strides he seemed to reach.
There at my pier his reindeer team he twitched
Loose from the pile to which they had lain hitched,
And clucking to them swung his whip; and they
Sped seaward out across the shining bay,
Beating the brine into a diamond dust
Beneath their hooves, while in a final thrust,
"Au revoir 25th December!" hoarse
His voice came back, and I—awoke, of course.

SORROW, MY SORROW

I

Sorrow, my sorrow, I thought that you would be
My faithful mate, and bear me company
While I should live, but now I find that you,
Like joy, and hope, and love, have left me too.

Sorrow, my sorrow, you have left me more
Forlorn than all the rest that went before;
For you were last to come and longest stay,
And you were dearest when you went away.
Sorrow, my treasured grief, my hoarded pain,
Where shall I turn to have you mine again?

II

Wherever there are other breasts that ache,
Wherever there are hearts are like to break,
Wherever there are hurts too hard to bear,
Turn and look for me, you shall find me there,
But not to take and have me for your own,
Or keep me, as you thought me, yours alone:
If you would have me as I used to be,
Beyond yourself you must abide with me.

CHRISTMAS

Youth, in the heart of faith now wearing old,
    Hope, in the darkness of this doubt and fear,
    Love, in the law inexorably severe,
Home, in the cosmic exile! I, in the cold,
Soon dusk of this my latest year, behold
    The beauty of thy coming, and the cheer
    Familiar, mystical, divine and dear,
Feel as in all the years that have been told.
About thy forehead and within thine eyes
    The innocent wisdom of the sage and child—
    Experience with expectance reconciled—
Shines, with ineffable prescience: the surmise
Of being, when the years no longer come,
Eternal in youth, and hope, and love and home!

EXPERIENCE

The first time, when at night I went about
    Locking the doors and windows everywhere,
After she died, I seemed to lock her out
    In the starred silence and the homeless air,
And leave her waiting in her gentle way
All through the night, till the disconsolate day,
Upon the threshold, while we slept, awake:
Such things the heart can bear and yet not break.

A SEASONABLE MORAL

The woman sang her ballad to the sky
Of the keen Christmas night, flinging on high
The notes that fluttered to my window-pane
Like birds, and beat against the glass in vain
Until I opened, and from out the gloom
Let them flock into my snug, firelit room.

There was no more of meaning in the words
That came than in the jargoning of birds,
But in the voice, and in the plaintive air
There was an intimation of despair
From killing sorrow, and the appealing cry
Of sorest need, which no man might deny
And cover from himself his own disgrace.
So, thoughtfully, as one does in such a case,
From among several coins in hand I chose
That of the smallest worth, and wrapped it close
In paper, so that it might not be lost,
Striking the frozen ground below, and tossed
My gift dwon from the window at the feet
Of the poor singer in the wintry street.

But she, as if she neither saw nor heard,
Rapt in her song, sang on, and never stirred,
While one, that opportunely strolled around
The corner nearest her, both heard and saw,
Stooped, and put out a predatory claw,
And clutched the paper; felt and recognized

The coin within (that somehow suddenly sized
My own soul up to me, in an odd way),
And then deliberately, but without stay
For all my frantic shouts and signs, kept on
To the next corner, turned it, and was gone.

What should I do? Let the poor singer go
Unhelped because of this misdeed? Not so!
Such a conclusion even I could not brook,
A coin of the same worth again I took,
Wrapped it again in paper, and again
Tossed it down to the singer—not in vain,
This time! She saw it coming through the air
And heard it fall upon the ground, and there,
While she still sang, curtseyed her thanks to me,
Until I turned away and left her free.

And I was well content, and glad at heart
For having doubly done a noble part?
I was not sure. Had it been heaven's intent
That I should twice give the sum I had meant
To give but once? Perchance, unknown to me
Both women were in equal misery,
Though not of equal merit. Then, had I won
A twofold blessing by what I had done?

These things are mysteries, but my story's moral
Seems one with which no one can justly quarrel:
If there is suffering that you would relieve,
Give twice the sum at once you meant to give;

And do not wait for wrong to come your way
And force your unwilling hand, for though it may,
Again, it may not, and, for your own sake,
The chance is such as you ought not to take.

ON A BRIGHT WINTER DAY

Foolish old heart, as glad of wind and sun
   And of the lift of yonder unclouded blue,
As if the world's delight had just begun!
   Do not you know such joy is not for you?

I know, I know! And yet I know that joy
   Like that which maddens in me from the day,
While yet I breathe must find me still a boy:
   Off, mocking Fear, and let the young heart play!

THE LITTLE CHILDREN

"Suffer little children to come unto me,"
Christ said, and answering with infernal glee,
"Take them!" the arch-fiend scoffed, and from the
    tottering walls
Of their wrecked homes, and from the cattle's stalls,
And the dogs' kennels, and the cold
Of the waste fields, and from the hapless hold
Of their dead mothers' arms, famished and bare,
And maimed by shot and shell,
The master-spirit of hell
Caught them up, and through the shuddering air
Of the hope-forsaken world
The little ones he hurled,
Mocking that Pity in his pitiless might—
The Anti-Christ of Schrecklichkeit.

THE PASSENGERS OF A RETARDED SUBMERSIBLE

THE AMERICAN PEOPLE

What was it kept you so long, brave German
submersible?
We have been very anxious lest matters had not
gone well
With you and the precious cargo of your country's
drugs and dyes.
But here you are at last, and the sight is good for
our eyes,
Glad to welcome you up and out of the caves of the
sea,
And ready for sale or barter, whatever your will
may be.

THE CAPTAIN OF THE SUBMERSIBLE

Oh do not be impatient, good friends of this neutral
land,
That we have been so tardy in reaching your eager
strand.
We were stopped by a curious chance just off the
Irish coast,
Where the mightiest wreck ever was lay crowded
with a host
Of the dead that went down with her; and some
prayed us to bring them here
That they might be at home with their brothers and
sisters dear.

We Germans have tender hearts, and it grieved us
    sore to say
We were not a passenger ship, and to most we must
    answer nay,
But if from among their hundreds they could some-
    how a half-score choose,
We thought we could manage to bring them, and
    we would not refuse.
They chose, and the women and children that are
    greeting you here are those
Ghosts of the women and children that rest of the
    hundred chose.

THE AMERICAN PEOPLE

What guff are you giving us, Captain? We are able
    to tell, we hope,
A dozen ghosts, when we see them, apart from a
    periscope.
Come, come, get down to business! For time is
    money you know,
And you must make up in both to us for having
    been so slow.
Better tell this story of yours to the submarines, for we
Know there was no such wreck, and none of your
    spookery.

THE GHOSTS OF THE *LUSITANIA* WOMEN AND CHILDREN

Oh, kind kin of our murderers, take us back when
    you sail away;

Our own kin have forgotten us. O, Captain, do not
   stay!
But hasten, Captain, hasten! The wreck that lies
   under the sea
Shall be ever the home for us this land can never be.

NOTES TO THE POEMS

THE IMPULSE TO MAKE THIS EDITION took first root in the perception that the poems organized as the poet first presented them look much more modern than they appear in *Stops of Various Quills*. Pursuing the poetry further, I came to see that the "Impressions," though Howells never segregated them, spoke strongly to one another when grouped according to the subtitle he gave them. And then the merest reading showed how much stronger the "Father and Mother" blank verse dialogues were in their first magazine texts, and finally it became clear that the long narrative poems belong together rather than shuffled with miscellaneous prose as in *The Daughter of the Storage*. The prime textual intent of this edition looks to enhance the poems by placing them in largely the texts Howells first selected for print. Notes to the poems discuss textual and other matters of relevance.

1. "Impressions"
It seems odd that no available record shows Howells commenting on the subtitles he placed on poems or on his titles for magazine groupings. It was not in Howells to be insensitive to such matters. Though he subtitled three of his best poems "Impression," he did not so gather them in *Stops of Various Quills* (hereafter *SVQ*).

2. "The King Dines"
PUBLICATION: *SQV,* XXXI
With its muscular imagery, forcible diction, and its desolating irony, "The King Dines" ranks as one of the best of Howells's poems. A distinguished representative of the literature of Boston Common, it applies to the condition of American homelessness even more powerfully than it applied when it was first published a hundred years ago.

3. "November—Impression"
PUBLICATION: *Harper's Monthly* (hereafter *HM*), November 1891,
906; *SVQ*, I. In *SVQ* the poems are numbered I–XLIII but not pagi-
nated.
TEXT: between the 1891 text and the *SVQ* there is a significant varia-
tion. The present text retains line 9 as it first appeared, rejecting the
revision in *SVQ* to "Of all the beauty, and of all." It cannot be known
whether Howells varied the text of his own motion or at editorial sug-
gestion; but it is rejected on the grounds that the revision scrambles
the syntax with its prepositional phrases now out of parallel and that
the introduction of the abstraction "beauty" is an error by the poet's
own standards. "Beauty" is so abstract as to seem "literose," and it veers
violently from Howells's pragmatic, psychological, and modernistic
line. "Beauty" belongs to the neo-platonic tradition of the unity and
parity of beauty, goodness, and truth which he had mocked in "The
Editor's Study" of December 1890. The first state of the poem, how-
ever, works in the mode of the other poems, often psychological,
often familial, which followed after the death of Winifred Howells.
    4. "Labor and Capital"
PUBLICATION: *SVQ*, XXXII
A period piece, with its dray-horse and driver imagery and old-
fashioned Socialist title, "Labor and Capital" speaks from the poet's
own time. Yet there is no way to evade the force of its irony.
    5. "Moods"
PUBLICATION: *HM*, March 1891, 608–9
The reason why Howells first published a titled gathering of his new
poems may only be guessed at. "Moods" announced the existence of a
new poetry. The modernistic title announced the character of the new-
ness. The emphasis on psychological experience keyed the poetry in
with Howells's current emphasis in fiction: *The Shadow of a Dream*
(1890), *An Imperative Duty* (1892), *The Quality of Mercy* (1892). "Moods"
proved so successful that the Harpers were heartened to engage
Howard Pyle as illustrator of collections to follow.
    6. "Another Day"
PUBLICATION: "Moods I"; *SVQ*, XXXVI
TEXT: In *SVQ* line 12 changed the earlier "most incommensurable
hope" to the better "farthest-reaching hope." The final ellipses are the
poet's.

7. "Life"

PUBLICATION: "Moods II"; *SVQ*, XXXVIII

8. "Temperament"

PUBLICATION: "Moods III"; *SVQ*, XLII

9. "Weather-Breeder"

PUBLICATION: "Moods IV"; *SVQ*, XXXIX

TEXT: *SVQ* line 1 reads "Oh, not to know." Insofar as there is a distinction between "Oh" and the "Ah" of "Moods," it seems to favor "Ah."

10. "Peonage"

PUBLICATION: "Moods V"; *SVQ*, XL

TEXT: In *SVQ*, line 7 is end-stopped with a comma; the lack of a comma after "blame" fits better with the context.

11. "Some One Else"

PUBLICATION: "Moods VI"; *SVQ*, XXXVII

12. "Monochromes"

PUBLICATION: *HM*, March 1893

"Moods" was a relatively new, psychological and yet common word; but "Monochromes" was technical, recondite, rather intimidating and "arty"—it smacked of the modern. It means about what the Greek roots suggest: plastic art-work done in one color, most often black-on-white. To see the first page in *Harper's* of "Monochromes" is to think that somehow Howard Pyle's illustrations suggested the title. "Question" ("Monochromes II") is surrounded on three sides by Pyle's black-on-white design. Pyle told Howells his designs were monochromes; or Howells recognized proofs as monochromes; or Elinor Mead Howells recognized proofs for what they were. The hypotheses are equally probable.

More important, the poems work in black-on-white and answer to the idea of "monochromes." Intense blackness runs through them; they focus on death, fate, loss; and the ironies never relent. Not a page is bright. Pyle spelled his sense of it out in the designs bracketing "Question": a *danse macabre* above with a placard saying "Melancholia"; a skull, surrounded by symbols of death and fate, below.

Relations between Howells and Pyle, while interesting, are not quite *à propos* to the present discussion. Pyle exercised no influence on the poems, which existed before his coming on the scene. The poems are strong, some of them among Howells's best, and Richard Watson Gilder of *The Century* wrote to say that he felt profoundly moved. E. C. Stedman anthologized "From Generation to Generation" and "Hope." He ought to have taken "The Bewildered Guest" and "Company" and "Living."

13. "Question"
PUBLICATION: "Monochromes I"; *SVQ*, XVI

14. "Living"
PUBLICATION: "Monochromes II"; *SVQ*, XII

15. "Company"
PUBLICATION: "Monochromes III"; *SVQ*, VI
TEXT: Line 2: Keep "have" from "Monochromes III."
LINE 8: Keep lowercase "w" in "why" from "Monochromes III."

16. "To-Morrow"
PUBLICATION: "Monochromes IV"; *SVQ*, XI

17. "Friends and Foes"
PUBLICATION: "Monochromes V"; *SVQ*, XXVIII
The famously amiable Howells had many personal friends and few if any personal enemies. Ideologically, he had plenty of allies and opponents, and these are the friends and foes of the epigram. For poetic success he exaggerated his alleged bitterness, however. He enjoyed the joke of his poetic neatness and, as O'Donnell found, inscribed "Friends and Foes" into gift copies of his novels.

18. "From Generation to Generation"
PUBLICATION: "Monochromes VI"; *SVQ*, IV
TEXT: *SVQ* places a "II" after the second stanza and italicizes the speech of the not yet born in stanzas 3 and 4, thereby helping the reader.

19. "The Bewildered Guest"
PUBLICATION: "Monochromes VII"; *SVQ*, V

20. "If"
PUBLICATION: "Monochromes VIII"; *SVQ*, XIII
TEXT: The poet changed the "Monochromes" title for this poem from "Hope" to the more ironic "If" in *SVQ*.

21. "Respite"
PUBLICATION: "Monochromes IX"; *SVQ*, XV

22. "Stops of Various Quills"
PUBLICATION: *HM*, December 1894, pp. 35–39. "SVQ" refers to the *HM* gathering; *SVQ* stands for the collected (1895) volume.

23. "Sphinx"
PUBLICATION: "SVQ, I"; *SVQ*, XXIX

24. "Twelve P.M."
PUBLICATION: "SVQ, II"; *SVQ*, VIII
25. "Time"
PUBLICATION: "SVQ, III"; *SVQ*, III
26. "Good Society"
PUBLICATION: "SVQ, IV"; *SVQ*, XXVII
TEXT: "SVQ" title was "Society."
27. "Heredity"
PUBLICATION: "SVQ, V"; *SVQ*, VII
28. "In the Dark"
PUBLICATION: "SVQ, VI"; *SVQ*, X
29. "Solitude"
PUBLICATION: "SVQ, VII"; *SVQ*, XIV
30. "Change"
PUBLICATION: "SVQ, VIII"; *SVQ*, IX
31. "Midway"
PUBLICATION: "SVQ, IX"; *SVQ*, II
32. "Conscience"
PUBLICATION: "SVQ, X"; *SVQ*, XX
33. "Calvary"
PUBLICATION: "SVQ, XI"; *SVQ*, XIX
34. "Pebbles" (hereafter "Peb")
PUBLICATION: *HM*, September 1895, 517–20
35. "The Burden"
PUBLICATION: "Peb"; *SVQ*, XVIII
36. "Hope"
PUBLICATION: "Peb"; *SVQ*, XVII
TEXT: *SVQ* line 4: "empty" replaces "Peb" "lonely."
37. "Sympathy"
PUBLICATION: "Peb"; *SVQ*, XXII
It seems likely that the play was Ibsen's *Ghosts*.
38. "Vision"
PUBLICATION: "Peb"; *SVQ*, XXV
39. "Reward and Punishment"
PUBLICATION: "Peb"; *SVQ*, XXI
40. "Parable"
PUBLICATION: "Peb"; *SVQ*, XXIV

Cf. Matthew 19:16–24. No doubt this also represents Howells's rejection of Tolstoyan example.

41. "Statistics"

PUBLICATION: "Peb"; *SVQ*, XXIII

42. Poems, 1891–1895

43. "What Shall It Profit?"

PUBLICATION: *HM*, February 1891: *SVQ*, XLIII

The first published in *Harper's*, this became the last in *SVQ*. Perhaps it was the least typical of the series.

44. "Mortality"

PUBLICATION: *HM*, May 1891; *SVQ*, XXXV

45. "The Wit Supreme, and Sovereign Sage"

PUBLICATION: *The New York Times*, May 1, 1892; copied by *The Critic*, May 7, 1892, p. 533: "A Unique Autograph Album"

A committee of the Press Club, conducting a benefit for the Actors Fund Fair, solicited "autograph" contributions from celebrities "in journalism or general literature," bound them "richly," and auctioned off the album.

46. "Judgment Day"

PUBLICATION: *The First Book of the Author's Club*, New York, 1893, p. 288

47. "Except as Little Children"

PUBLICATION: *Fame's Tribute to Children*, ed. Mildred S. Hill (Chicago, 1893), Part 2, p. 24

Howells wrote his "autograph sentiment" to be published in holograph for charity.

48. "Race"

PUBLICATION: *HM*, April, 1894; *SVQ*, XLI

49. "Society"

PUBLICATION: *HM*, March 1895; *SVQ*, XXVI

50. "Equality"

PUBLICATION: *SVQ*, XXXIII

In the early 1890s Howells came forth as a supporter of women's rights and freedom, especially in his "Altrurian Essays." A lover of theater, even of vaudeville and the circus, he had to consider matters of sexual display and exploitation. The poem suggests that it is a matter of equality if women exploit male sexuality as men exploit feminine sexuality. Both are equally complicit to the point where exploitation and complicity end in solidarity: death.

51. "Scene and Story"

52. "Materials of a Story"

PUBLICATION: *HM*, May 1892; *SVQ*, XXX

Howells the later poet was mostly a novelist. Thus "Materials" became a story and a realistic one (thus a realistic poem) in spite of its title. Thus it qualifies for inclusion in the section of "Scene and Story."

53. "Breakfast Is My Best Meal"

PUBLICATION: *Frank Leslie's Popular Monthly*, August 1899; *The Daughter of the Storage* (hereafter *DS*), 1916

Done not in dialect but in Middle Western vernacular, "Breakfast" reflects the popular revolt against cosmopolitanism and the machine age. Howells did "take the cure" at Carlsbad for his dyspepsia. Hungry and bored, he found an imaginative revenge in "Breakfast" and won a popular success with it.

54. "Father and Mother: A Mystery"

PUBLICATION: 1. *HM*, May 1900; 2. *The Mother and the Father. Dramatic Passages*, New York, 1909

55. "City and Country in the Fall: A Long-distance Eclogue"

PUBLICATION: *Harper's Weekly* (hereafter *HW*), November 29, 1902; *DS*

56. "The Mother"

PUBLICATION: *HM*, December 1902; *The Mother and the Father*, 1909

57. "Black Cross Farm (To F.S.)"

PUBLICATION: *The Spectator* (London), January 2, 1904; *DS*, 1916

Bibliographically, "Black Cross Farm" eludes discovery even more successfully than the lost, enigmatic place that is its subject. Its magazine publication and date became one of the exceedingly few lacunae in Gibson and Arms. No historian has accounted for its escaping the Harpers and finding first publication in an English journal nor identified "F.S." It is true that, with the award of Howells's Litt. D. Oxon. in June 1904, his reconciliation with England rose as high as it ever would. John St. Loe Strachey, editor of *The Spectator*, had earlier sought and won Howells's friendship. And it was true that his relations with the Harpers were then dicey. There are reasons to suppose that he offered "Black Cross Farm" to the *Monthly*, which refused it, so he offered it to Strachey, who was charmed. The *Monthly* did not print any of the other long narrative poems; but it did take the "Dramatic Passages," the Father and Mother poems.

58. "After the Wedding"

PUBLICATION: *HM,* December 1906; "The Father and the Mother" in *The Mother and the Father,* 1909

Given Howells's method with novels, it is conceivable that he sold the idea of the volume to the Harpers before he wrote (not later than the summer of 1906) "After the Wedding." Mark Twain read the poem in manuscript in June 1906, when it was obviously work in progress.

59. "The Face at the Window"

PUBLICATION: *HW,* December 14, 1907; *DS,* 1916

TEXT: There is one significant textual variant. In *DS* line 145 reads, "How perfectly New England!" and that revision is accepted.

During the same general period as "The Face at the Window" Howells had been publishing the tales collected in *Questionable Shapes* (1903), and would follow by collecting *Between the Dark and the Daylight* (1907). As no one has quite explained, Henry James and Mark Twain were also deep in composing stories of the supernatural in the same period. The story behind "The Face at the Window" Howells seems to have first heard from his brother Joe, which could mean that it began as a Lake Erie yarn. Something may have been suggested by Kipling's *Captains Courageous* (1897). But for New England character Howells had plenty of material at home.

60. "Captain Dunlevy's Last Trip"

PUBLICATION: *DS,* 1916

For "Captain Dunlevy . . . " and its background see Cady, "Howells on the River," *American Literary Realism, 1870–1910* (spring 1993): 27–41.

In "Dunlevy" there are echoes from "The Pilot's Story," 1860, and the radical essay "Floating Down the River on the O-H-I-O." I think it a good guess that Howells began the poem not long after he wrote the essay but pigeon-holed it until 1915 as O'Donnell's notes suggest.

61. "Contemporaries"

62. [To John Burroughs]

PUBLICATION: Not previously printed. Quoted in mimeograph in *The Howells Sentinel.* Original in Barrett Collection, University of Virginia. The original is A.L.S. on a calendar page for May 11, 1909. Why Howells wrote it on or near that date is not clear. Burroughs had praised Howells in a review of *Criticism and Fiction* (*Critic,* February 6, 1892). They stood on warm personal terms, as is evident from Howells's freedom in 1903 to josh Burroughs about planning to go to Yellowstone with Theodore Roosevelt and "hold bears for the President to shoot" (*Life in Letters* 2:170).

The narrow calendar sheet presents a question regarding the proper lining of the quatrain. I think the common form the best choice.

63. "A Double-barrelled Sonnet to Mark Twain"
PUBLICATION: *HW,* December 13, 1902
Why the Harpers celebrated Clemens's sixty-seventh birthday at a big New York dinner on November 28, 1902 is not clear. At any rate, Howells's double sonnet led off the poems prepared for the occasion.

64. "The American Joke"
PUBLICATION: as "Sonnet to Mark Twain," *HW,* December 23, 1905; revised, as "The American Joke," *My Mark Twain,* 1910
Introduced after the reading of a letter from President Theodore Roosevelt, Howells was called "the most fitting person in all the world to perform the task." In response he began:

These cheers, Mr. President, and ladies and gentlemen, are more terrifying to me than the dead silence of which I would gladly be a part. Since you have thought me fit, I could not wish a greater pleasure than that which you have proffered to me. I have written something prefatory to the toast I shall propose, and I wish before reading it to offer you what I believe ought to be a biographical explanation. Mr. Clemens has always had the effect on me of throwing me into a poetic ecstasy. (Laughter.) I know it is very uncommon. Most people speak of him in prose, and I dare say there will be deal of prosing about him to-night; but for myself, I am obliged to resort to metre whenever I think of him. I fancy there is some strong undercurrent of poetry in the man which drags me down and sweeps me along with him. I remember three years ago, when he was a comparative youth of sixty-seven, I was called upon to respond to some sort of toast, and I instantly fell into rhyme. I don't know that I shall quite be able to scramble out of it tonight. At that time I praised him in what I ventured to call a double-barrelled sonnet; it was a sonnet of twenty-eight lines instead of fourteen. To-night, as he has reached the Psalmist's age limit, I thought perhaps a psalm would be more fitting; the psalm of David, if we could not get anything better. (Laughter.) But I found myself quite helpless when it came to the matter of preparation, and I fell back on the Shakespearean sonnet. I found myself, however, obliged to write a Shakespearean sonnet of extraordinary length. Shakespeare wrote sonnets of fourteen lines, mine is of twenty-eight. But you will find Shakespeare again has been improved upon since he died. Mr. Bernard Shaw now writes plays twice as good as Shakespeare—and I write sonnets twice as long as Shakespeare. (Laughter and applause.) I don't know that I need delay you longer from the pleasure before you, but such as my sonnet is, I will read it. This is a sonnet to Mark Twain.

The second state of the text looks like a clarification of the *Harper's Weekly* version that looks like a copy from a reporter's shorthand notes.

65. "To a Great Editor" [Henry Mills Alden]

PUBLICATION: "To the Editor of Harper's Magazine on his Seventieth Birthday," *HW,* December 15, 1906, p. 1812

Though tensions between Alden as editor and Howells as a contributor have sometimes been dramatized by commentators, personal relations remained cordial—even to the point of collaboration. Howells admired the poet and man of soul in Alden.

66. [Thomas Bailey Aldrich]

PUBLICATION: not previously published. T. F. O'Donnell found it at the Houghton Library, Harvard.

When Howells came to work for the *Atlantic* in 1866 he met a rollicking friend and competitor also employed by James T. Fields. Aldrich edited the magazine *Every Saturday.* He and Howells became "generational" friends: contemporaries who enjoyed each other's wit and giftedness for a decade and then, still friends, drifted apart, grew apart intellectually and esthetically. Much the same happened between Aldrich and Mark Twain.

After Aldrich's death in 1907, his wife, a stuffy and snobbish lady, insisted on an "Aldrich Memorial" event, commandeering both Howells and Clemens to write and read at the service their tributes. Somewhat sardonically, both complied. (See *Mark Twain—Howells Letters,* 2:831). The present poem, though the better of the two Howells wrote for Aldrich, he apparently held back.

67. "Aldrich, 1866–1907"

PUBLICATION: Not previously published. The date January 15, 1910, at the foot of the other Aldrich tribute may suggest either that Howells made a fair copy of the Memorial poem or else that for some reason he thought the second and less personal poem better suited to Mrs. Aldrich's intention to frame the poem to place beside Howells's photo-portrait on the wall. At any rate, T. F. O'Donnell found the poem at Harvard.

68. "[Joseph A. Howells]"

PUBLICATION: *Life,* 2:323

Howells's older brother fancied having the imposing stone of the *Ashtabula Sentinel,* the family newspaper, used to mark his grave. It turned out to be fortunate that Mildred Howells, his younger daughter, preserved the verses, because the stone did not hold up well against the frosts of the Western Reserve and has long been almost illegible.

69. "Poems: 1902–1916"

70. "The Christmas Spirit"

PUBLICATION: *HW,* December 6, 1902

On August 17, 1902, Howells playfully wrote to his sister Aurelia, "I find myself inclined, in my autumnal years, to the poetry I thought would make my fame when I was young." (*Selected Letters,* 5:34). He anticipated the cornucopia to appear in December. Mark Twain, a grateful recipient, summed it up in a letter dated "Xmas-Eve/02": "I read to people—I praised—the pair of birthday poems ['The American Joke'] & the Santa Claus poem, & the deep and moving one which you wrote at York ['The Mother']."

"The Christmas Spirit" (the "Santa Claus poem") pleased both Howells and Clemens for its thrusts at the new American imperialism, which both condemned.

71. "Sorrow, my Sorrow"

PUBLICATION: *HM,* December 1903

72. "Christmas"

PUBLICATION: *HW,* December 12, 1903

73. "Experience"

PUBLICATION: *HM,* May 1904

74. "A Seasonable Moral"

PUBLICATION: *HW,* December 10, 1904

75. "On a Bright Winter Day"

PUBLICATION: *HM,* November 1913

76. "The Little Children"
PUBLICATION: Edith Wharton, ed., *The Book of the Homeless [Le livre des sans-foyer]*, 1916
Howells's old friend Henry James solicited a contribution to Wharton's war-relief volume. See Michael Anesko, *Letters, Fictions, Lives: Henry James and William Dean Howells* (New York, 1997), pp. 461–65.

77. "The Passengers of a Retarded Submersible"
PUBLICATION: *The North American Review,* November 1916

INDEX OF POEM TITLES AND FIRST LINES